W9-CBR-695

DATE DUE

NOV 7

NOV DE

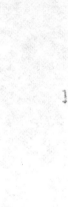

The
Old Testament
and
Criticism

by

CARL E. ARMERDING

WILLIAM B. EERDMANS PUBLISHING COMPANY
GRAND RAPIDS, MICHIGAN

Copyright © 1983 by William B. Eerdmans Publishing Company
255 Jefferson Ave. S.E., Grand Rapids, MI 49503

Library of Congress Cataloging in Publication Data
Armerding, Carl Edwin.
The Old Testament and criticism.

Includes indexes.
1. Bible. O.T. — Criticism, interpretation, etc.
2. Evangelicalism. I. Title.
BS1171.2.A75   1983   221.6'01   83-1629
ISBN 0-8028-1951-6

·Contents

I. AN EVANGELICAL OLD TESTAMENT
   CRITICISM? 1
   Introduction 1
   **The Word of God, the Words of Men, and the
   Critical Task** 4
      Traditional Conservative 4
      Rational Critical 6
      Evangelical 7
      History, Revelation, and Inspiration 11
   **The Old Testament and Various Forms of
   Criticism** 15

II. LITERARY CRITICISM 21
   Introduction 21
   Purpose 22
   Method 23
   Literary Criticism and the Documents 28
   Criteria for Separating the Documents 29
      Divine Names 29
      Doublets 32
      Differences in Detail 36
      Theological Viewpoint 37
      Style 39
      Summary 41
   Conclusion 42

III. FORM CRITICISM 43
   Introduction 43
      Definition 43
      Origin 44
      Relation to Revelation 45

v

Method   49
Define the Unit   49
Describe the Genre   50
Determine the Life-Setting   52
Determine the Function   54
**Further Examples of an Evangelical Form
Criticism**   56
Prose Genres   56
Poetic Genres   59
Prophetic Speech   61
Critique and Summary   63
Benefits   63
Cautions   63

IV. STRUCTURAL ANALYSIS   67
Introduction   67
Structural Analysis: The Discipline   69
Professional Semiology   69
Propositions and Assumptions   70
Method   72
Synchronic and Diachronic Research   72
Steps in Structural Exegesis   74
Other "Structural" Methods   78
Literary Approaches and Structural Analysis   84
Structural Analysis in the Pentateuch   86
Recent Approaches   89
Summary and Conclusions   92
What is Structural Exegesis?   92
Structural Analysis and the Quest for Meaning   93
Conclusion   96

V. TEXT CRITICISM   97
Introduction   97
Development of the Old Testament Text   100
Early Period   100
Masoretic Period   107
Hebrew Texts and English Versions   112
Hebrew Texts   112
English Versions   114

Contents

Kinds of Textual Errors 119
Unintentional Changes 119
Intentional Changes 123
Rules for Text Criticism 125
Summary 127

Indexes 129

I

An Evangelical Old Testament Criticism?

INTRODUCTION

FROM the days of such men of piety as George Adam Smith and James Orr in Scotland, or C. F. Keil and Franz Delitzsch in Germany, evangelical students of the Old Testament have struggled with the question of biblical criticism. There is no avoiding the fact that in the years since Julius Wellhausen of Greifswald published his *Prolegomena zur Geschichte Israels*,[1] commitment to some form of a critically reconstructed Old Testament (OT) has become a new scholarly orthodoxy. Those who resisted the tide, such as C. F. Keil, a Lutheran professor and prolific writer in Dorpat, have been largely forgotten by contemporary scholarship,[2] despite the fact that almost one hundred years after his death his major works are still in print. On the opposite side, men like George Adam Smith, who combined devotion and rational criticism (to the dismay of their conservative constituencies) are still remembered, frequently as heroes in the struggle against obscurantism. Even those who do not show the evangelical piety of Smith often cite his work as a pioneering example of the triumph of critical method. In the middle stood men like James Orr and Franz Delitzsch. Considered hopelessly conservative by their colleagues in the "enlightened" critical world of the Scottish and German universities, they are still seen by many

---

1. Originally published as *Geschichte Israels* (Berlin: Georg Reimer, 1878), and from the second edition onward under the title *Prolegomena zur Geschichte Israels* (Berlin: Georg Reimer, 1883); Eng. trans. *Prolegomena to the History of Israel*, trans. J. S. Black and Allan Menzies (Edinburgh: Adam & Charles Black, 1885).
2. *Die Religion in Geschichte und Gegenwart*, 2d ed., 5 vols. (Tübingen: J. C. B. Mohr, 1927-31), typically omits his name.

1

conservative scholars as having granted concessions to a rationalistic methodology which in the end could only lead to Wellhausen's conclusions.

The issues persist today. They affect not only the evangelical scholar seeking to preserve viewpoints which radically separate him from his more liberal colleagues, but virtually every student of the OT as well. University lectureships are given on the basis of adherence to critical thought, and textbooks are judged by the extent to which they affirm the current brand of critical orthodoxy, while popular television programs disseminate the latest theories to the waiting masses.

Traditionally, conservative Christians have argued that the question of authority is at stake. To submit to OT critical methodology would be to admit that the Bible can be studied as a merely human book. A critical approach implies human criticism of the authority of the revealed Word of the Lord from heaven. To preserve that authority the Bible must contain a trustworthy historical record, and to preserve the integrity of that record there must have been a fairly simple literary and textual process of formation, with an early acceptance of the final product by the community. A very conservative approach to the dating and authorship of OT books was seen as a necessary concomitant to the authoritative role of a divinely inspired Word.

Together with a rejection of critical methods, the conservative rejected the rationalism that characterized many (but not all) early critics. The critic could argue that prophecies like the Cyrus oracle of Isa 45:1 demand a late Isaiah; the conservative replied that God could and did reveal even names of later kings when He spoke to and through His prophets. The critic might arrive at a late date for 1 Kgs 8, basing his claim on a highly developed view of God in the chapter; the conservative could reply that Solomon received his understanding of God by revelation, and no naturalistic framework was required to explain it. Again, the critic might argue that Deut 17:14-20 was post-Solomonic, for it mentions kings, horses, and harems. To the conservative, however, the problem did not exist: God had revealed the law to His servant Moses, who then transmitted it in writing; God knew of Solomon's future propensities, and that was enough.

But today a question remains: Are rationalistic presuppositions, to which conservatives rightly objected, a necessary part of critical methodology? Is it possible to hold a traditionally conservative or high view of revelation and still affirm the basic methods of the critic? Or is it true, as many older liberals and conservatives agreed, that critical thought and a supernatural Bible are antithetical? If so, the problem becomes a simple matter of theological presuppositions. We can choose to believe in a divinely inspired Word of God and reject rationalistic criticism, or we can accept the rationalism of the critic and assign to the Bible the status of a merely human book. At least, these are the terms in which the issue is generally presented today.

But is the antithesis necessary? Must one be a rationalist, and reject the concept of revelation, to study adequately the OT? Conversely, does a high view of Scripture carry with it ready answers to the questions which are raised by critics concerning text, date, authorship, and style? Can a conservative, with an evangelical view of revelation and the inspirational process, hold open questions of authorship, date, and literary history? An article by an evangelical scholar has questioned the alignment of conservative theology with conservative criticism. John Goldingay argues openly for accepting the Bible's authority, inspiration, and infallibility, while rejecting as a corollary to this commitment a necessary adherence to traditional approaches to critical questions.[3]

I would like to go back and examine various views of revelation and inspiration, in order to see what it is about these views that has made critical methodology seem so offensive. In doing so, we must also look at critical method, to ask if that discipline can be practiced apart from certain rationalistic presuppositions that have been unacceptable to evangelicals. We must clarify what is an evangelical view of revelation, that is, how and in what sense the Bible is the Word of God. From that point we must further ask what conclusions about critical method follow from this view of revelation, and how they intersect with criticism as it is commonly practiced in biblical studies today. Is it possible to employ critical method, but reject some of the assumptions which lie beneath it? I suggest that it is — that conservative theology both permits and even demands the use of the best critical

---

3. John Goldingay, "Inspiration, Infallibility, and Criticism," *The Churchman* 90 (1976):20; cf. idem. *Approaches to Old Testament Interpretation*. Issues in Contemporary Theology (Downers Grove: Inter-Varsity Press, 1981).

tools, but that the way these tools and methods are used may differ sharply at the point of presuppositions from the way the same tools and methods are employed in the hands of a rationalistic critic. Our point of departure is an examination of the way in which we understand the Bible to be the Word of God.

THE WORD OF GOD, THE WORDS OF MEN, AND THE CRITICAL TASK

Let us begin by looking at three ways of viewing the Bible: two are somewhat extreme, and a third represents a *via media*, or a middle path. The first is that of the traditional conservative who rejects critical methods out of a conviction that the Bible is the Word of God. The second is that of the traditional rationalist who rejects special revelation out of a conviction that the Bible is merely the words of men. The *via media* is that of an evangelical critic — a scholar who attempts to account for the high view of the OT held by Christ and the New Testament (NT) apostles, but who is fully aware that the words of God come in human forms, thought patterns, and literary structures.

Traditional Conservative

The terms "traditional" and "conservative" are here not intended as pejorative; they function, rather, as helpful appellatives to describe a shade of opinion which differs from what I shall suggest as a more evangelical view. A traditional conservative holds that the Bible is so purely the Word of God that it almost ceases to be in any meaningful sense the words of men. The view is usually linked by its critics to some form of dictation theory of revelation, though it is difficult to find a Christian apologist who defends what so many are alleged to hold. Calvin employed the term, but only as a "theological metaphor"[4] to describe "the work of the Holy Spirit in relation to the part played by the human authors,"[5] rather than in any sense of mechanistic psychology.

---

4. J. I. Packer, "Calvin's View of Scripture," in *God's Inerrant Word: An International Symposium on the Trustworthiness of Scripture,* ed. J. W. Montgomery (Minneapolis: Bethany Fellowship, 1974), p. 103.
5. Ibid., p. 102. See further Kenneth Kantzer, "Calvin and the Holy Scriptures," in *Inspiration and Interpretation,* ed. John F. Walvoord (Grand Rapids: Wm. B. Eerdmans, 1957), pp. 137-42.

But apart from the mechanics involved, it has been possible for many conservative scholars to hold in practice a view in which the Scriptures are so totally the Word of God that consideration of any critical question save that of textual corruption is seen as illegitimate. Thus any meaningful discussion of post-Mosaic elements in the Pentateuch, any attempt to find human life-settings for the Psalms, or any question of literary growth in the prophets is viewed as tampering with a sacred text. From this position, God is seen as directly involved at every stage of the revelatory process, and its adherents are at home with the concept of "original autographs," on the assumption that here we find the locus of direct divine inspirational activity.

Many a scholar who functions from this perspective, whether Christian or Jew, has fruitfully employed the tools of textual, linguistic, and historical criticism. In addition to these scholarly apologists, there arc unfortunately numerous men and women whose ideas on the Bible are largely obscurantist, and many of those also hold a fundamentalistic concept of revelation and inspiration. But we are not discussing popular aberrations: the true conservatives, in the best sense of the word, are persons whose scholarly training and apparatus are second to none; they simply believe, on the basis of a high view of Scripture, that questions of style, authorship, and date can be settled in favor of very traditional positions. They often know a great deal about history, archeology, philology, and science, but their views on the nature of the Bible invariably produce a rejection of any form of what they feel to be destructive critical endeavor. Even when they argue on purely rationalistic grounds, their conclusions are predictably conservative.[6] I believe it is important to recognize that this view is concomitant to a particular understanding of the nature of revelation and the inspirational process. In other words, the very limited use of critical tools results directly from a conviction that these tools have been employed to the advantage of a wrongheaded theology.

---

6. E.g., W. J. Martin, *Stylistic Criteria and the Analysis of the Pentateuch* (London: Tyndale Press, 1955); D. J. Wiseman et al., *Notes on Some Problems in the Book of Daniel* (London: Tyndale Press, 1965); Gleason L. Archer, *A Survey of Old Testament Introduction* (Chicago: Moody Press, 1964); E. J. Young, *An Introduction to the Old Testament*, rev. ed. (Grand Rapids: Wm. B. Eerdmans, 1964). See the comments of James Barr, *Fundamentalism* (London: SCM Press, 1977), pp. 124-25.

Rational Critical

A second extreme views the Bible in purely human terms, that is, as no more than a record of Israel's thought and life. In one sense, grouping all the adherents of this view under the rubric "rationalist" is not accurate, for the class includes those who hold to no doctrine of revelation together with many whose ideas of revelation are other than evangelical. In the latter category are scholars of both liberal and neo-orthodox persuasion, for whom the revelatory activity of God is a step or two removed from the kind of direct inspirational work of the Holy Spirit claimed by the conservative or evangelical. Men like Gerhard von Rad of Heidelberg, or G. Ernest Wright of Harvard, argued for a God who did reveal Himself, whether in the history of Israel, in the very human and erring responses of the people of God, or finally and fully in Christ and the NT Church. But in another and limited sense, their doctrine of Scripture is not unlike that of the true rationalist, that is, the one who believes that there is neither God nor revelation. The OT for such theologians does not represent in any direct or supernatural form the Word of God. Neo-orthodoxy has argued for the Word of God as revelation contained in, or heard through, the Scriptures, but the Bible itself remains a purely human response. No specific saying of a prophet, no particular law handed down through the cult, no expression of praise or wisdom can be pointed to with a clear affirmation that "This is the Word of God." If any writers of Scripture seem to exhibit powers of observation, discernment, or knowledge above their own natural ability, this phenomenon is seen as at best a secondary, rather than direct or primary, influence of the Holy Spirit.

With such a view, the words and thoughts of Scripture are, in effect, read as merely human words and thoughts. The OT is a record of Israel's thought and life — her response, in forms of varying value, to God and the influences around her. To such a book the canons of secular rationalistic criticism are applied without special favor. Factual as well as theological errors are discerned in the text, for its nature as a record of human thinking implies the inevitable presence of error. Whether or not the critic believes in divine revelation, the methods will be about the same. The task of a critic — in contrast, say, to the task of a biblical theologian — is not so much to discover normative truth as to

6

determine the process by which the writing arrived at its present state, and then to determine the influence it had on its own time. Specifically supernatural interventions of the Holy Spirit as an explanation for any given phenomenon are neither sought nor accepted. Thus, the criticism of this group is, in the final analysis, a criticism from purely naturalistic presuppositions. As with the traditional conservative, these assumptions guide the critic: the former may refuse to recognize an element that calls for explanation in normal historical or literary terms, while the latter may with equal conviction explain on other grounds an element which the text relates to direct divine disclosure or activity.

Evangelical

In calling this position evangelical, I must acknowledge that it is a view of revelation theoretically shared by many whose critical approach is either traditionally conservative or liberal critical. In making the distinction, I have attempted to square various concepts of revelation with their respective implications for critical method. At that point, a large group of biblical critics function, in effect, like fundamentalistic traditionalists or rationalistic liberal critics, whatever view of revelation they actually affirm.

This third view sees the Bible as the Word of God in the words of men. There is really no distinction that can be made between the two—Scripture is totally the Word of God even as it comes totally in the words of men. This means that evangelical critics will desire, like traditional conservatives, to guard against setting aside marks of special revelation or supernatural intervention. It also means that, like liberal critics, they will be genuinely open to the flow of history, the cause-and-effect relationships of human progress, and the literary forms in which these are expressed. To understand how evangelicals work out this tension, and see exactly how their doctrine intersects with various aspects of biblical criticism, we will have to take a closer look at what the evangelical understands by "The Word" and "the words."

First, the Word of God in Scripture is both event and proclamation; that is, God's Word comes both in His mighty acts and also in the speech of prophets and apostles. When God acts in history, that activity may take the form of making a path in the depths of the sea for the redeemed to cross over (Isa 51:10), or it may come in the form of a word burning in the heart of a prophet (Jer 20:19); in either case, it is a vital, divinely inspired force (Isa 55:11). There is a constant interplay between the Word and the words. Sometimes the proclaimed word brings about the working of God's will, as in His command to Jonah, "Arise, go to Nineveh, that great city, and cry against it" (Jon 1:2). That word, incarnate in Jonah's flight, return, proclamation, and bitterness, finally brought about the repentance and consequent preservation of the city. It was Jonah's word, in the last analysis, just as much as it was God's. As with every true prophet, the distinction cannot be maintained.

Sometimes the word of the prophet follows and explains the act. When Moses and the children of Israel sing a song on the shore of the Red Sea (Exod 15), the evangelical hears in the song a divinely ordered response to a divinely caused event. Each is, in a unique sense, revelation. Both the words of Moses and the act of God are Word of God. But an evangelical can also study the song as the words of Israel. In fact, in reading the song, an evangelical critic may find evidence of response on more than one level. Vv. 1-12 celebrate the act of God just seen at the sea, but vv. 13-18 seem to go beyond the event at the sea. These verses celebrate the perpetual kingship of Yahweh, and are more appropriate as the liturgy of a people in the land than as the liturgy of a band of newly freed slaves at the Red Sea. The evangelical is able to consider the possibility of a combined narrative with several levels of transmission, but cannot separate out one level from another to find which is Word of God and which are words of men. God has been supernaturally at work in all of Israel's history, and the response to His working, at whatever stage, becomes a part of His Word when incorporated into the inspired narrative. How evangelicals use the song, and what kind of doctrine, reproof, correction, or instruction they will take from it is a hermeneutical question, but their doctrine of revelation views the entire song as Word of God.

Within such a framework, what kind of criticism can be applied? Can the evangelical critic hold to the inspired nature of the song as a commentary on God's mighty act, and still find in the completed hymn elements of a much later liturgy of the Jerusalem temple? Can one discern marks of literary development without violating a commitment to the inspiration behind the text? At yet another level, can the evangelical follow contempo-

8

rary critics and find, not only in the Song but in the event itself, the product of a long chain of traditional development? If the words of Scripture are truly human words and can be studied as such, what are the controls which the evangelical view of revelation places on the study? I would like to suggest that evangelicals do have controls which inform their approach, just as much as traditionalists and rationalists. As conservative Christians, with a high view of the Word of God, evangelicals are committed to the truth-value of Scripture. If they do find a chain of development in Exod 15, they do so only with the conviction that the development is part of the inspirational process, and in no way affects the truth-value of the text or its message. If they undertake a study of the historical value of the reported event—the drying up of the Red Sea—they do so in the belief that supernatural acts in history can and do take place, and that these are evidence of God's Word in the world. If their investigation convinces them that the text does not intend them to believe that the event literally occurred, they are open to criticize the historical base of the narrative, but their commitment to a revelational theology in the very words of Scripture (verbal inspiration) controls both what they believe can happen with regard to a reported miracle and the truth-value of the record as it has been received.

What then are the ingredients for an evangelical criticism? I would like to suggest that a moderately critical approach is fully consistent with the view of revelation set out above. Evangelical critics can and will use all the tools provided by literary and historical science, but they have definite controls. Perhaps another look at Exod 14 and 15 from this perspective will help to illustrate the point.

Exod 14, as a third-person narrative with a theological conclusion (vv. 30-31), seems to have been composed by someone other than Moses, at some time after the event. Exod 15, a poem in which the salvation of God is celebrated in three stanzas directed successively against Pharaoh's army, the forces of the sea, and the enemies in Canaan, seems a clear telescoping of various salvation oracles with similar themes. The job of the literary and form critic is to analyze the parts and determine how the final form was reached. Evangelical critics will have no theological objection to the basic method, but they may not share certain positivistic presuppositions with the more rationalistic critics. A criticism which has concluded before starting that an event like the rolling back of the Red Sea by direct divine intervention cannot happen in history is not the criticism of an evangelical. That kind of criticism looks at the narrative not to discover its history *since* the event, but to find out *how* the incident was invented and developed. Evangelicals, in contrast, are free to look at the narrative in Exod 14 without this restriction. Their criticism is directed to discovering how and in what forms the narrative developed.

In a similar fashion, evangelicals can look at the poem in Exod 15 as true literary critics. They believe God did something real at the sea, and can perceive in the poem that this event has become, under the superintending influence of the Holy Spirit, a normative picture or model for other saving events. They not only expect people to celebrate that event in various ages, but in the form of their celebration they discern the guiding hand of God's Holy Spirit. As a result, evangelical critics have no problem with a possible telescoping of events. They hold that God has given the impetus, in a direct sense, for this combination. Their role as critics is merely to discover the process, in order to understand better the working of God.

In such an approach, neither the Word of God nor the words of men are lost. The conservative critic believes that the Lord does fight for His people (Exod 14:14), and that this principle is both illustrated and celebrated by our example. Not only Moses but later generations as well used the event at the Red Sea to rejoice in the God of their salvation. In the ongoing process of salvation history, some of their words became the settled forms in which God's Spirit would communicate the truth and meaning of that event to succeeding generations. This has become, for us, a true revelation of a genuine event. God has become one of us, He has taken the fleshly form of human history and mortal words, and meets us at that point. There is no longer any distinction between the Word of God and the words of men, for this identification comes at the end point of the process, the point at which the community of faith recognized in the set forms of the speech the Word of God. The evangelical critic, however, does not bring naturalistic presuppositions even to the question of when these forms were settled. Moses' own words can as well form the canonical Word as those of later generations — there is no a priori. A long process of transmission is not required, nor does it weaken the force of the original word or event, since the process is divinely guided.

History, Revelation, and Inspiration

What we have just described is fully consistent with a classical evangelical understanding of history, revelation, and inspiration that differs at significant points from the other theological systems described above. Let us summarize the nature of an evangelical position and its distinctive points for each category.

History. The biblical narrative treats events of Israel's past as history, not mythology, for what happened to Abraham onward, and even prior to Abraham all the way back to creation, took place in a time-space continuum. Its world and its people are the world and people we know today. Ancient mythology, while holding a great deal in common with the world of today, deals primarily with creatures and events of a different order. The nearest analogy in the biblical narrative is the Serpent in the Garden of Eden, though even there the LORD God is carefully described in nonmythological terms. The task of the historian is to discover, record, sift, evaluate, and interpret the facts and events.

In the case of mythology, the problem is not with the validity of events as described but with their accessibility. The events of myth lie outside the realm of the historian's investigative machinery. We simply cannot check whether the Egyptian gods Horus, Seth, and Osiris took certain forms and performed certain acts in their celestial realm.[7] Here the myth is designed to picture a timeless primeval order, removed completely from the stuff of which history is made. In the same way, we are limited in our investigation of Babylonian creation mythology. The earth, as we know it, appears relatively late in the story, and mankind is incidental.[8] By contrast, in the Genesis account, prehistoric though

---

7. See, e.g., a text on "The Primeval Establishment of Order," trans. John A. Wilson, "Egyptian Myths, Tales, and Mortuary Texts," in *Ancient Near Eastern Texts Relating to the Old Testament*, ed. J. B. Pritchard, 3d ed. with supplement (Princeton: Princeton University Press, 1969), pp. 9-10.

8. "The Creation Epic" (also known as *Enûma eliš*), trans. E. A. Speiser, "Akkadian Myths and Epics," in Pritchard, *Ancient Near Eastern Texts*, pp. 60-72.

it is, the world which appears is immediately our world, and Adam and Eve are at the center of the process.

The task of the critic, then, is the task of the historian. Like the historians of antiquity, who sifted and evaluated the past from the perspective of their own time and its values, the historians of today look back to the past with their own perspective on reality. As biblical critics, Christian historians use all the tools of historical investigation, but also recognize in Israel's life and literature a phenomenon that is unique—a revelatory history. The phenomenon of a history which is in a special sense revelatory does not put that history outside the realm of investigation, for it would then no longer be history. It demands, rather, that the critic-historian prepare to recognize in this unique history, and in the literature which expresses it, a special kind of reality.

Mythology, which by modern standards is less real, is the opposite. Divine history, for the Christian, is more real because it takes into account at every point the reality which is God as He reveals Himself to His world. But, and this is the key point, in contrast to their treatment of the myth, biblical critics can never dispense with the tools of their historical craft. The reality, or super-reality, of God's revelation is so genuinely a part of humanity and its past that it would be unthinkable to study it without critical tools.

Revelation. The foundation of Christian theology, as Leon Morris has rightly pointed out, is the self-disclosure of God.[9] True, Christians have not always concurred on how this was done, but normally it would still be agreed that we cannot reach a knowledge of God unaided. The relationship between revelation and the Bible is, for this discussion, a pivotal point. If God revealed Himself directly and uniquely in the events and persons who acted out and wrote Holy Scripture, then we are bound as critics to take this into account. The real point at issue is this: Does the revelation or self-disclosure of God directly as well as indirectly influence events, persons, and thoughts? Traditionally, the Christian has affirmed that it does, or at the very least, that it did in the Bible.

For evangelical critics, this affirmation is a watershed. In no

9. Leon Morris, *I Believe in Revelation* (Grand Rapids: Wm. B. Eerdmans, 1976), p. 11.

sense does direct supernatural intervention allow them to dispense with critical tools, for revelation comes in the form of historical events and literary expression. In fact, this affirmation adds a new dimension. The Christian critic, standing before God's revelation, realizes humbly that there are events and knowledge that may not be fully understood by normal laws of cause and effect. For example, we may study ancient ideas of creation as a normal growth of a certain kind of intellectual history. When we come to the Bible, we can study its cosmogony (creation story) as part of the world of antiquity, but if we believe God has revealed Himself in Gen 1–3 we expect to find a new and possibly inexplicable element. In other words, Christian critics do not simply try to explain a natural process; they look for and expect to find a supernaturally given insight, often contradicting the natural.

At precisely this point, the criticism of the past 150 years has often been at variance with conservative theology. Conservatives believe in revelation of a particular kind because they believe this is the Bible's own teaching regarding revelation. Therefore, they can allow for ideas which are "too advanced for their time" or events which seem to violate the natural order. Their critical knives need not be applied to excise all such elements, as in the case of their more positivistic colleagues. As a result, conservative critics are free to examine the process of tradition and transmission without the limitations of the rationalist. They would agree that revelation normally comes in a cause-and-effect historical sequence, as one can see in the historical nature of the biblical material, but they can also look for another element.

We thus live admittedly in a tension. Our God is not one who suddenly and capriciously intervenes at surprising intervals, upsetting the course of history and rendering all investigation fruitless. Quite the opposite. The God of both OT and NT is presented as Author and Sustainer of the natural order. Thus the Christian can study not only history and literature, but science as well. The medieval alchemist's principle is not essentially Christian, though the alchemist had a handle on a half-truth which many an intellectual of today has missed, namely, that God could intervene in His world if He so chose. What the alchemist failed to see was God's normal working order within which He had ordained us to live. It is precisely in the normality of the established order that God has primarily revealed Himself. But the biblical view would, in addition, affirm a second principle. The same God who created the normal order directs it to His own ends, and must be left free to intervene in its processes. Thus we have the possibility not only of miracles but of new and expressly revelatory concepts. The creation account is but one example; the giving of the law on Mt. Sinai is a more direct (and therefore unusual) case of the same principle at work. Christian critics, because they believe in revelation, can study both of these events without explaining them away.

Inspiration. 2 Tim 3:16 speaks of a Scripture which is *theópneustos,* that is, God-inspired or God-breathed. It is often held that this process forbids the application of literary and historical tools to the reading of the product. But the description, far from establishing the Bible as a kind of uncreated Book dropped suddenly into a hostile world, emphasizes only the fact of the Bible's resultant authority. There is no hint that the inspirational process has created a monster (literary or otherwise) from outer space, free from the restraints of normal communication mechanisms or literary forms. Rather, because the Bible is in some sense God breathing His thoughts, concepts, and even words through and into human agents, the resulting product is "profitable for teaching, for reproof, for correction, and for training in righteousness, that the man [*ánthrōpos*] of God may be complete, equipped for every good work." This inspiration, like revelation, assumes the normal processes of history and communication, but adds an additional dimension. This dimension will be taken into account by Christian evangelical critics — they will bow before what they find. They will let it teach them, reprove them, correct them, and instruct them in righteousness. But they can no more dispense with the tools of the critic in seeking to understand it than they can in reading any other ancient book.

Summary. Heb 1:1 sums up, in brief, what we have been saying. First, "God spoke." Thus the OT, in a special and unique sense, is a revelation. We are not dealing merely with human responses to events but with the voice of God. A believing criticism must take this into account. Second, He spoke "by the prophets." The revelation came through or within (*en*) human writers. It becomes a part of the normal literary process of communication. It is not on tablets suddenly dropped from heaven or dug up in a New York meadow. The prophets "moved by the Holy Spirit spoke from God" (2 Pet 1:21), but it was they who spoke. The book is thus fully human as well as fully divine. "In many [*polymerōs*] and various ways [*polytrópōs*]": as B. F. Westcott has phrased it, "the variety . . . extended both to its substance and to its form. The great drama of Israel's discipline was divided into separate acts; and in each act different modes were employed."[10] Here we have a sense of the variety of form and the unfolding or progressive nature of the revelation that so marks the earlier Testament. The reader must be both literary critic and historian. The question, as we have seen, is not whether we shall apply critical tools, but how. Heb 1:1 gives the balance. Criticism is a must, but the presuppositions with which we employ it will vitally affect the outcome of its application.

THE OLD TESTAMENT AND VARIOUS FORMS OF CRITICISM

The OT is a book of history and literature. Furthermore, it is an old book, written at a time and in languages far removed from our own. It is a book formed in various and disparate ways, most of which involved some process of transmission. Even after a part of the OT had assumed a set form, usually connected with its taking on an authoritative role, the writing continued to be copied and disseminated. As a result, this total process determines the kinds of critical tools we must employ.

Text criticism. The text of the OT, like that of any book of which we possess only later copies, presents various problems. Sometimes a reading is not clear or seems to be grammatically improbable, and we suspect an error in transmission. At other points there may be specific evidence of variant readings in the Hebrew, or in the Greek and other versions. Again, copyist errors (such as writing the same phrase twice or omitting the second of two original phrases) are patently evident. The task of the text critic is simply to ascertain the original form of the writing, and

10. B. F. Westcott, *The Epistle to the Hebrews* (1920; reprint ed., Grand Rapids: Wm. B. Eerdmans, 1974), p. 5.

this is done with a variety of tools according to well-established procedures. Christians, like Jews before them, have always engaged in this discipline, and now with the publication of the Dead Sea Scrolls, the field in OT studies is broader than ever. For the first time in almost a thousand years, we have new manuscripts in the Hebrew language, and much of the work in their evaluation remains to be done.

Linguistic criticism. The linguistic critic studies words and phrases and their relationship to each other. For a book written in an ancient tongue, long dead despite the preservation of many of its forms through the years, the task is much more complicated. In addition to the traditional role of the philologist, recent studies in linguistics indicate that an entire field of anthropology (structural analysis) must inform the study. But the traditional role of the philologist is not thus rendered unnecessary; it is merely made more difficult and taken forward another step. Christian scholars, including those with the highest views of revelation and biblical authority, have always engaged in this kind of research.

Historical criticism. In its simplest form, historical criticism is little more than what the Reformers meant by grammatical-historical exegesis. It constitutes inquiry into whatever local or historical factors may have shaped the biblical message. For many critics of the modern era, historical criticism also involves an application of historical criteria to various biblical texts in order to determine their age, sometimes from an understanding of history that is too rigidly evolutionary. Evangelical criticism must certainly utilize all the historical research available, but it should maintain a proper caution in the face of any theory of history that is superimposed on the text. Perhaps the greatest need among evangelical historians is not to elucidate the background of the text but to articulate a Christian philosophy of history and show how redemptive history fits within it.

Comparative religions criticism. Comparative religions research (*religionsgeschichtliche methode*) begins with an assumption that the religion of the OT is best understood by analogy to ancient religions in general.[11] Such a presupposition must be rejected on the basis of an evangelical view of revelation, and many of the conclusions of the comparative religionists will be unacceptable to believing Christians. But despite the limitations of such a method, it is apparent that a study of the religious aspects of ancient society will illuminate many practices within the history of Israel. In this sense, comparative religions research becomes a part of historical criticism and is regularly employed by conservative scholars.

Source or literary criticism. G. E. Ladd defines literary criticism as "the study of such questions as the authorship, date, place of writing, recipients, style, sources, integrity, and purpose of any piece of literature."[12] The conservative is of course as concerned about date, authorship, style, and so on as any other Christian. In OT studies, this inquiry is often called source criticism, for literary criticism was traditionally identified with an attempt to discover the written sources of the OT books. Although challenged by the newer science of form criticism, literary criticism has retained its role as the study of the process by which the text developed into its present written or literary form. While conservative critics can remain quite unconvinced by older theories like the so-called Graf-Wellhausen hypothesis (which was based on a certain evolutionary view of Israel's development), they can never abandon the study altogether. One of many examples will suffice. In Gen 1 and 2 we have parallel, supplementary, or possibly conflicting accounts of aspects of creation. Both are literature, but even a hurried reading will uncover considerable differences of style, if not of content. The evangelical critic, while not limited to naturalistic theories, will certainly want to pursue the literary questions which are raised.

Form criticism. Unlike the literary critic, the form critic is concerned with the oral or preliterary history of a text. Succinctly defined by G. M. Tucker, its purpose is "to relate the texts before

11. George Eldon Ladd, *The New Testament and Criticism* (Grand Rapids: Wm. B. Eerdmans, 1967), p. 196. Ladd provides a brief, lucid summary of the school and its method.
12. Ladd, *Criticism*, p. 112.

us to the living people and institutions of ancient Israel."[13] The definition presupposes that many texts, or portions of texts, originally arose in a setting other than the obvious context of the passage or book, and that the effort to trace the saying or section backward in time is both possible and profitable. While conservative critics may blanch at the subjectivity implicit in much of this work, they must nevertheless face the evidence that many texts or portions of texts did circulate orally. The critic, while retaining a healthy sense of his own limitations, will find that a search for settings and roots, though not the most important part of his study, can make a fruitful contribution. Evangelicals have profited greatly from form-critical studies in the Psalms, and have themselves contributed several major form-critical studies, especially in Deuteronomy.[14]

Structural analysis. A more recent interest of biblical scholars has shifted the focus of study from the history of the text up to its final stage to the history of the text *since* its final stage. Building on certain theories of linguistics, structural analysis looks at the finished text as a whole to discover beneath its surface the "deep" structures in the society or author that not only shape the text but are embodied within it. In a sharp departure from traditional approaches to criticism, the structural analyst also works with structures operating in the readers and in their views of reality. Much of the work in this field is too recent to evaluate, and structuralists are still sorting out exactly what they mean by the term, but already it is clear that some great gains have been made in the study. That the final form of the text is a more fruitful field for study than various putative stages of its history is an idea which comes like a breath of fresh air. Believing scholars, certainly no less than their colleagues, must be interested in the mysterious process of communication and language. What the Bible says to modern man has always been of prime concern

13. Gene M. Tucker, in the Preface to *Form Criticism of the Old Testament*, Guides to Biblical Scholarship, Old Testament Series (Philadelphia: Fortress Press, 1971), p. xi.
14. See, e.g., Meredith G. Kline, *Treaty of the Great King* (Grand Rapids: Wm. B. Eerdmans, 1963); idem, *The Structure of Biblical Authority*, rev. ed. (Grand Rapids: Wm. B. Eerdmans, 1975); K. A. Kitchen, *Ancient Orient and Old Testament* (Chicago: Inter-Varsity Press, 1966), pp. 90-102; cf. J. A. Thompson, *The Ancient Near Eastern Treaties and the Old Testament* (London: Tyndale Press, 1964).

to the evangelical, and this aspect of critical work claims to elucidate the process.

Canon criticism. Another approach which challenges the historical dimension of the critical task has been called canon criticism. In OT studies, this is normally thought of as a study of the Scriptures in the context of a canonical affirmation of the believing community. That is to say, the most important point about the text may not be its prior history but the theological role played by the text as part of a broader whole in the context of the community which affirmed its normative status.[15] Obviously an attractive field for evangelical endeavor, canon criticism as a method has now been applied in a major commentary on Exodus by its chief advocate, Yale theologian Brevard S. Childs.[16]

Summary. By now it should be evident that evangelical scholars must also be biblical critics. In the sense that I have described it, criticism is not itself a negative or destructive science. The tools of criticism, in the hands of a scholar committed to the views of Scripture taken by Christ and the apostles, can be used to great advantage in gaining a better understanding of the OT. Such a view of revelation may limit the type and extent of critical endeavor, but it can never eliminate the need for critical studies. Indeed, evangelical critics may be more free to engage in creative work, for only their view of revelation can take account of the full activity of the living God described in the biblical text. We can use all the tools of historical, philological, and literary study while still retaining biblical categories of revelation, inspiration, and history. The advantages of this combination should be valued and pursued.

15. G. T. Sheppard, "Canon Criticism: The Proposal of Brevard Childs and an Assessment for Evangelical Hermeneutics," *Studia Biblica et Theologica* 4, no. 2 (1974):3-17.

16. Brevard S. Childs, *The Book of Exodus: A Critical, Theological Commentary,* Old Testament Library (Philadelphia: Westminster Press, 1974).

II
Literary Criticism

INTRODUCTION

LITERARY criticism, as practiced by critics within various sub-disciplines of the literary world, is described in *Encyclopaedia Britannica* as the art of judging qualities and values of an aesthetic object, in this case a work of literature.[1] The same article suggests that criticism should consist of the application of principles of literary composition, including the rules of writing. The definition presupposes a basis of principles which determine correctness and quality of literary expression, and these the critic may apply in order to evaluate a written product.

But this is not specifically what is meant by literary criticism of the OT. Certainly it bears some relationship to the discipline described above, but "literature" as used today is conceived of more broadly as the entire body of written remains from a given society. This latter understanding of the term informs the role of the literary critic in a biblical sense, for biblical literature cannot always be classified as *belles lettres*. The biblical critic, then, is not as exclusively concerned with aesthetics, or even with communication, as is his counterpart in the literary community.

In OT studies, literary criticism has from the beginning been associated with the discovery of literary patterns, and these, in turn, enable the critic to isolate various sources. From a study of sources (begun especially in the eighteenth century), this inquiry further developed an interest in the authorship, date, unity, style, setting, and intent of each source. Traditionally, biblical scholarship had concerned itself with two disciplines: establishing the best text of a given passage, and then determining its mean-

1. *Encyclopaedia Britannica*, 1945 ed., 4:727.

21

ing. The former discipline was called "criticism," and the latter "hermeneutics." With the rise of OT source analysis, the terms "lower" (for textual) and "higher" (for literary) criticism began to be used. The higher critic went beyond the text to ask questions about its authorship, background, and source. Because a host of subcategories is currently practiced within the field of biblical criticism, it is probably best to use the term "source" or "literary" criticism for the discipline as a whole.

The OT corpus is not literature only in the sense that it represents Israel's written legacy, for it does contain literature of the highest aesthetic quality. But the OT literature, with all its varied forms, is unique and noteworthy mainly as a collected body of writings, produced in two languages, over a period of perhaps six hundred years, by various authors known and unknown. As a result, not only questions of style and content but also of authorship, dating, intent, and development have inevitably been raised. When the French physician Jean Astruc published his theory about pentateuchal sources in 1753,[2] his was not a new inquiry. For many years men and women in both Jewish and Christian circles had speculated about the origin and development of certain books. Although he apparently never went so far as to question Mosaic authorship of the final product, Astruc went behind the individual books to suggest that a literary history could be discerned for component parts of each. Modern OT literary criticism was born.

Today many new questions have somewhat superseded the older literary criticism. In particular, form criticism (which deals more specifically with the preliterary stages of a given text) has brought a recognition that the problems are far more complex than older literary critics were aware. But literary criticism of the OT, despite a host of modern modifications, is still viewed by many as foundational to OT studies, and for this reason must be given its share of our attention.

PURPOSE

Norman Habel suggests that the purpose of literary criticism is

2. Jean Astruc, *Conjectures sur les mémoires originaux dont il paroit que Moyse s'est servi, pour composer le Livre de la Genèse* (1753); see a discussion and the literature cited in Otto Eissfeldt, *The Old Testament: An Introduction*, trans. Peter R. Ackroyd (New York: Harper & Row, 1965), pp. 160-62; R. K. Harrison, *Introduction to the Old Testament* (Grand Rapids: Wm. B. Eerdmans, 1969), pp. 498-99.

"to provide the literary spadework for a better understanding of the function and import of a document."[3] He points out, moreover, that our commitment to the message of the OT urges the use of every available tool to discern the full meaning of the biblical text.[4] As we proceed, we must ask in what sense and to what extent the methods and conclusions of traditional literary criticism in fact lead us to a better understanding of the "function and import" of the text. Evangelicals will naturally ask whether a direct study of the text in its final form does not accomplish this purpose better, and the question is currently echoed by some of the most advanced thinkers in the critical field. Nevertheless, on the premise that any knowledge of the Bible is helpful, and in view of the promise which literary criticism shows of furthering that knowledge, we shall proceed with the inquiry.

METHOD

In studying the text, the literary critic attempts to discern the following: (1) clear structural or internal arrangements; (2) clear themes, and how these are developed; (3) the extent and literary history of separate units, if any; and (4) the stylistic features of those units which can be isolated. To illustrate this enterprise, let us examine Gen 1 and 2, for these chapters have frequently formed a basis for literary-critical analysis.

In Gen 1 may be observed a structural arrangement according to the seven days of creation, or to the ten utterances of God. The passage is in fact so easy to outline that we suspect the writer was concerned to communicate a sense of orderly development. The universe begins as a formless mass and is progressively developed in response to divine fiat (the Word of God) in seven stages. The climax of this activity is the creation of man, who is represented as vice-regent of earth under a transcendent God. The account reaches a second peak in 2:1-3 where the Sabbath, or seventh day, is set aside to represent God's final rest following the work of creation.

What are the themes of this section? First, the Creator is

3. Norman C. Habel, *Literary Criticism of the Old Testament*, Guides to Biblical Scholarship, Old Testament Series (Philadelphia: Fortress Press, 1971), p. 7. The work provides a brief, up-to-date guide to source criticism of the OT.
4. Ibid.

clearly a God who is a step removed from His creation (contra ancient Near Eastern myth),[5] although His link with the world is well defined. His Word creates all things, while man, in His image, is given dominion over all, such that God is not left without a witness to Himself. In addition, this God is a God of order, and all that is made bears the stamp of its Maker: order emerges from chaos, pattern from the random, structure from the fluid. His world is good, and He can rest with the work completed.

These themes run throughout Gen 1:1 – 2:3 in a way that is quite consistent with the structural features noted above. As we shall see, however, not only the themes but the entire literary structure changes from 2:4 onward, so in isolating the literary unit we stop at 2:3. From the data already presented, it is reasonably clear that we are looking at a unified, coherent literary production, marked by a common structure and a thematic unity. Such a clarity is not always available, of course, and I have deliberately chosen a lucid example for that reason.

Finally, what about stylistic features? Claus Westermann finds a basic rhythm, a kind of heavenly liturgy, in the passage, the movements of which he summarizes under five headings. First there is an announcement, "And God said . . . ," followed by the commandment, "Let there be . . . ," and the report, "And it was so." After each report there is an evaluation, "And God saw that it was good," and finally, the temporal framework, "And there was evening, and there was morning, the . . . day."[6] This structure exhibits a fairly common vocabulary, a settled form, and stabilized transitional terminology. A number of additional stylistic features which mark the chapter have been isolated,[7] but these lie outside the scope and purpose of the present study.

Gen 2:4-25 (and probably chaps. 3 – 4 as well) is very different. The style is narrative, with the measured cadence of chap. 1 replaced by the epic suspense of the storyteller's skill. We are carried back in 2:4b to the day that the LORD God made earth and heaven, and immediately introduced to a problem: there are no plants, no rain, no man to work the ground. The story pro-

5. See, e.g., Nahum Sarna, *Understanding Genesis* (New York: Schocken Books, Schocken Paperback ed., 1970), pp. 11-12.
6. Claus Westermann, *The Genesis Accounts of Creation*, trans. Norman E. Wagner, Facet Books, Biblical Series 7 (Philadelphia: Fortress Press, 1967), pp. 6-7.
7. Some of these are outlined in Habel, *Literary Criticism*, pp. 22-27.

ceeds with the creation of the required man, and all is placed in subordination to him. The Word of God is not, as in chap. 1, the agent of creation, but the LORD God more directly forms and shapes, plants and gives breath. A search for clear structural or internal arrangements is not rewarded with anything comparable to the day-by-day unfolding of chap. 1, for the narrative comes to a close at the end of chap. 2 and a shift in subject matter occurs at the opening of chap. 3. Chap. 2 is plainly a separate literary unit.

Clear themes are developed in chap. 2 as in chap. 1. If the transcendence of God is stressed in chap. 1, the nearness of God to His creation is an emphasis of chap. 2. While man and woman are seen as the climax of a cosmic creation in chap. 1, the man is set over against all creation in his uniqueness as a social being in chap. 2. Here the environment is his environment, the productivity of the world and its beauty are his to enjoy, the labor of the world is his to perform, and the companionship of the woman is his to share. Chap. 1 presents creation in a general way; chap. 2 focuses on man and his relationships.

On what basis can we say that chap. 2 is a literary unit? Are there any smaller units within the chapter? Here, as in chap. 1, there is no substantial difficulty. Gen. 2:4-25 simply presents itself as a narrative unit. Different as it is from chap. 1, it has obvious unity and integrity as a story from beginning to end. The question is not whether 2:4-25 constitutes an independent unit, but whether this unit stops at the end of chap. 2. The subject matter changes, but similar structural and stylistic features continue.

What are these stylistic features? In addition to the epic style, cast in the form of a drama, we have the obvious (and sometimes overstressed) fact that Gen 2 and 3 (but not 4) use the term LORD God (Yahweh Elohim) for the Deity. Chap. 1, in contrast, always refers to the Deity by the generic title Elohim alone. But there are other stylistic differences, of which perhaps the most obvious relate to differences in creation terminology. Unlike the God who creates (*bārā'*) by His word, the LORD God of Gen 2:4-25 is more like a potter, a smith, or a farmer in His mode of activity. The differences may be explained in a variety of ways, but the job of the literary critic is merely to note them at this point.

What of the fact that we find here two distinct literary units? Traditionally evangelical or conservative scholars have viewed chaps. 1 and 2 as complementary, as parts of a larger whole that structurally fit into a continuous narrative running through Gen 11.[8] In the present form of the text this is no doubt true, but the differences we have noted need not, for this reason, be ignored or brushed aside. Clearly we have two separate literary units. So the questions remain: how do we account for their origin and distinctiveness, and what role does their study play in our understanding of Genesis? One modern evangelical, Derek Kidner, while holding to an early date for the book as a whole, is ready to posit a number of sources, both oral and written. He contends, however, that "the mechanics of composition are matters of small importance, since the parts of this whole are not competing for credence as rival traditions."[9]

To this point in the analysis, there is little on which critics would differ, but we now come to the point of greatest divergence between traditional conservative and liberal criticism. Kidner evaluates the mechanics of composition as "matters of small importance," while for Habel they provide "the literary spadework for a better understanding of the function and import of a document." We must press him for elucidation of the method that goes beyond the literary analysis already presented, but meanwhile other questions remain. What makes the difference between the views represented by Kidner and Habel? Can the two views be reconciled?

Briefly, the difference lies in what Habel and traditional source critics do next with the data we have outlined from Genesis. Habel links Gen 1 and 2 with two respective traditions or documents which OT scholars, despite recent reservations, still designate the Priestly (P) and the Yahwistic (J) traditions. For the older literary critics, separation into documents was the key to

---

8. E.g., William H. Green, *The Unity of the Book of Genesis* (New York: Charles Scribner's Sons, 1895), pp. 2, 9, 15; H. C. Leupold, *Exposition of Genesis*, 2 vols. (1942; reprint ed., Grand Rapids: Baker Book House, 1976), 1:105; E. J. Young, *An Introduction to the Old Testament*, rev. ed. (Grand Rapids: Wm. B. Eerdmans, 1964), pp. 50-51; H. G. Stigers, *A Commentary on Genesis* (Grand Rapids: Zondervan Publishing House, 1976), p. 64.

9. Derek Kidner, *Genesis: An Introduction and Commentary*, Tyndale Old Testament Commentaries (Downers Grove: Inter-Varsity Press, 1967), p. 22.

understanding the Pentateuch: Gen 1 (P) was believed to represent a theological viewpoint and related interests whose origin was not from Moses and his time but from the priestly circles in the Babylonian Exile or later. Gen 2 (J) was viewed as part of a great narrative epic revealing Israel's beliefs at the time of David or later. The theology of each was distinct, as was its form. Kidner, on the other hand, represents the standard conservative critic. No less aware of the differences between Gen 1 and 2, he does not agree that these are best accounted for by positing two or more great documentary sources.[10] This particularly when these documents are linked to a reconstruction of Israel's history — the developmental hypothesis — that purports to date their theological ideas according to either an evolutionary or a Hegelian dialectical understanding of how these ideas unfolded. Contemporary critics, in turn, are inclined to grant the weakness of the developmental hypothesis, but they still hold to the general hypothesis of documentary sources. Habel is perhaps representative: his book closes with the suggestion that "these hypotheses [the dates of J and P] are secondary, however, to the new insights into the diverse motifs, interpretations, thought progressions, theologies, and messages which are unveiled by the discipline of literary criticism as applied to the Pentateuch."[11]

I would like to take up Habel's last point and press the issue, for it removes a considerable barrier to the use of literary-critical methods, a barrier which has historically given hesitation to those holding the more traditional view of revelation as outlined above in Chapter I. If the entire schema of dated documents, accompanied by its varying theologies, is no longer the key to literary criticism of the OT, let us set the grid aside and move on to the "new insights" promised by the method. That there are separate forms and discernible literary styles within the OT literature is clear; that they represent a dialectic of later developing theologies is less than certain. Every attempt to discern or construct a set of absolute criteria which would isolate an entire document has ended in an unrewarding fragmentation of the text, or sharp

10. Kidner, *Genesis*, p. 58.
11. Habel, *Literary Criticism*, p. 84.

differences of opinion as to what was represented in each.[12] In some contrast, however, the kind of analysis that has taken each literary unit as a whole, and analyzed it in terms of (1) its internal structure and theological thrust, and (2) its role or place in the larger structure of the present text, has produced real fruit. For example, as we have seen, Gen 1 and 2 are very different literary productions; each tells its own story and stresses its theological themes in a unique way. The final editor of the book used these sources to create the great theological document we call Genesis, which contains and combines various theological strands. Without literary analysis we should lose something of the rich diversity of these documents, but let us not spoil the literature by rigidly tying its underlying documents or traditions to an evolutionary scheme which is foreign to the text itself.

LITERARY CRITICISM AND THE DOCUMENTS

We have seen how even the most conservative critic is forced to study the OT as a collection of literary works, and yet how this fact in no way compromises his doctrine of revelation and inspiration. Why then have conservative scholars so consistently rejected what was called literary criticism by its OT practitioners? We have suggested that the reason is related to the documentary hypothesis and its foundational role in traditional application of the Graf-Wellhausen method. Even a brief glance at modern undergraduate textbooks will show that the hypothesis, although modified at many points, is still presented as the most reasonable solution to problems of diversity in the Pentateuch. In addition, although the documentary theory as now taught applies specifically to the Pentateuch only, the method behind it is often applied to the entire OT canon. It is imperative, then, that we look at the reasons why a simple analysis of literary patterns has led to such a tenacious commitment to a schema like the JEDP reconstruction of the Pentateuch.

To follow through on our analysis of Gen 1 and 2, we find in a book like Habel's an extrusion of the criteria applied to the

---

12. Critiques of the method are essayed by Umberto Cassuto, *The Documentary Hypothesis*, trans. Israel Abrahams (Jerusalem: Magnes Press, 1961); O. T. Allis, *The Five Books of Moses* (Philadelphia: Presbyterian and Reformed Publishing Co., 1943); Cyrus H. Gordon, "Higher Critics and Forbidden Fruit," *Christianity Today* 4 (1959):131-34.

opening chapters. His second section both utilizes what we have seen and extends the method to find evidence for two different groups of material running through Gen 1–9. It is the element of literary continuity in the accounts, sometimes at the expense of the unity of the present text, that Habel (following a long tradition) uses to set the stage for introducing the concept of two original documents, namely, the Yahwistic and the Priestly. Gen 1 and 2 was an easy place to begin, for the criteria clearly emerged from a study of the text, but what about the next step? Do chaps. 1–9 break down so clearly, and is there enough evidence to assert without qualification the presence of two separate and parallel accounts?

I should like to begin by reviewing the criteria generally employed to separate documentary strands; some of these were already applied to Gen 1 and 2. But now the question is not only whether we can isolate literary units, but also whether there is sufficient evidence to construct a theory of sources. It should be noted that many contemporary form critics prefer to speak not of documents in a literary sense but of the special character of various kinds of literature. Thus Gerhard von Rad can isolate J, E, and P strands but see them as ways of thinking which culminated in blocks of tradition.[13] The final result, however, still places the blocks of tradition on the side of what we earlier criticized as a nonsupernaturalist view of revelation. In this sense, von Rad is only a step removed from many of the older adherents to the documentary hypothesis.

CRITERIA FOR SEPARATING THE DOCUMENTS

Divine Names

Historically, the J and P documents were first separated according to varying use of the divine names. We have seen how strictly Gen 1 and 2 differ in their employment of Elohim (God) and Yahweh Elohim (the LORD God) respectively. If the matter were always so simple there would be no reason why the criterion should not be employed throughout the Pentateuch. But already in chap. 3, while the narrative portions retain the combination

13. Gerhard von Rad, *Genesis: A Commentary*, trans. John H. Marks, Old Testament Library, rev. Eng. ed. (London: SCM Press, 1972), pp. 24-28.

LORD God, the quotations by the Serpent and the woman revert to the name Elohim (vv. 1-5), supposedly a mark of the E or P strand. Chap. 4 changes the form again, now to Yahweh (LORD) alone, except for the quoted speech of Adam's wife in 4:25, where Elohim is used. We can seek to account for the data in several ways. Chap. 1, after all, seems to constitute a literary unit on other grounds, and similarly 2:4–4:26. We can look at each independently and analyze its style, perhaps finding a clue to the varied usage within each unit. In fact, the variants within 2:4–4:26 might be best accounted for by the statement in 4:26 that "At that time men began to call upon the name of the LORD [Yahweh]." But we still have no proof that the names can be used to distinguish separate documents or literary strands.

Chap. 5 contains only five references to the divine name, all of which are Elohim. It is for this reason frequently related to chap. 1, but we must again ask if the other criteria for matching two literary works may be consistently applied.

In chaps. 6–9, the matter becomes more complicated. Now we are no longer working with clearly defined literary units but with a continuous narrative which source critics have been forced to divide in a way hardly warranted by the text. Using various criteria including that of the divine names, critics have generally agreed, with minor variations, that the Yahwist was represented by Gen. 6:5-8; 7:1-5, 7-8, 10, 12, 16b-17, 22-23; 8:2b, 6-12, 13b, 20-22; and the Priestly version by 6:9-22; 7:6, 9, 11, 13-16a, 18-21, 24; 8:1-2a, 3-5, 13a, 14-19; and 9:1-17. This is quite different from what we have been doing in that to this point we have worked only with the literary units received in the text itself.

But to remain with the criterion of divine names—how does the theory fare? In the division just given, made originally on the basis of the divine names, the separation into sources is fairly clear. But several points should be noted.

(1) The theory requires what may seem to most readers, especially those familiar with other ancient epics, the unnatural mutilation of a given story. This is admittedly an individual value judgment, but the traditionalist has in his favor the force of the text as it stands, while the source critic must show that the combining of strands of various documents was in fact done in the world which gave rise to the OT literature.

(2) The criterion does not account for Gen 6:1-4 or 9:18-29,

in both of which the divine names are mixed. S. R. Driver labels 6:1-4 and 9:18-27 as J, and 9:28-29 as P.[14] It should be noted, however, that this analysis cannot be made on the basis of the divine names without fragmenting the text beyond repair.

(3) In the case of Gen 7:16, the criterion of divine names — and only this criterion — forces a division in the middle of a sentence. The previous "J" section, v. 12, provides little context for the statement "and Yahweh shut him in," which fact led Driver to rearrange the text and put 7:16b after v. 9.[15] But, and here is the point, v. 16b fits well after 16a, except for the problem of the divine name. Is it not better to follow Cassuto and look for another reason for the distinction between the names?[16]

(4) On the one hand, Gen 7–9 is perhaps the easiest place in the Pentateuch to make a division based on divine names. On the other hand, Allis specifically cites Gen 24:15–30:24 (the narrative about the birth of Jacob's sons), where a division on the basis of names results in considerable fragmentation of the text.[17] In a modern commentary, von Rad can observe only that "this piece is composed of small parts, in places very small fragments, of J and E."[18] These divisions do no justice to the integrity of a given literary creation, and call into question the application of this particular method.

(5) A final point on divine names is the witness of textual variants: ancient versions of the OT exhibit enough variation in their use of the names of God to introduce further doubt about the method.[19]

In summary, we can say that the variant usage of divine names is a clear and useful criterion in analyzing the literature of Gen 1–4, though exactly what the force of the usage may be (whether literary or theological, for example) is open to debate. In Gen 6–9, however, the application of this criterion leads to an undesir-

14. S. R. Driver, *The Book of Genesis*, Westminster Commentaries, 11th ed. (London: Methuen & Co., 1920), pp. 82, 108, 111.

15. Ibid., p. 118.

16. Umberto Cassuto, *A Commentary on the Book of Genesis*, trans. Israel Abrahams, 2 vols. (Jerusalem: Magnes Press, 1964), 2:91-92; cf. Allis, *Five Books of Moses*, pp. 35-39.

17. Allis, *Five Books of Moses*, pp. 25-26.

18. Von Rad, *Genesis*, p. 293.

19. See chap. 2 of Harold M. Weiner, *The Origin of the Pentateuch* (London: Elliott and Stock, 1910), and a reply in John Skinner, *The Divine Names in Genesis* (London: Hodder and Stoughton, 1914), e.g., pp. 1-2, 4, 89, 104-105, 160-63.

able fragmentation of the text, and is itself difficult to apply with any consistency. It becomes an uncertain criterion upon which to build a theory of sources or documents running longitudinally through the Pentateuch.

Doublets

A second criterion used by literary critics to separate or discern underlying sources is the presence of doublets, or parallel accounts, in the text. It must again be stressed that analysis of doublets is not the sole province of the source critic: any student of literature will be aware of parallelisms of various kinds, and know that they may either obscure or clarify the message of the particular literary medium in which they are found. In the OT, as in the NT, there are lengthy narrative sections which give parallel accounts of the same event, or series of events. A study of Samuel-Kings, for example, will require comparison of its content, style, omissions, inclusions, and theological themes with the parallel material in Chronicles. The same is true of poetry. Not only have we certain poetic sections which are duplicated (e.g., 2 Sam 22 and Ps 18), but portions of psalms and prophetic utterances are reflected in other contexts (e.g., Hos 8:14b and Amos 2:5). The student of literature will evaluate each of the parallels in its context, attempt to trace the lines of dependence and interrelationship (does Hosea reflect a theme from Amos, or vice versa?), and use the parallel to illuminate the text with which he is working.

An example from the life and career of David according to Samuel and Chronicles will illustrate the point. The Chronicler was clearly working with sources, one of which was probably the Samuel-Kings account, but he omits a great deal and includes other material which is not found in Samuel. Parallel, but with important differences in detail, are the records of Nathan's prophecy regarding the Davidic dynasty (2 Sam 7 = 1 Chr 17), a list of David's triumphs (2 Sam 8 = 1 Chr 18), the victory over the Ammonites (2 Sam 10 = 1 Chr 19), and the narrative in which David numbers the people (2 Sam 24 = 1 Chr 21). Unique to Samuel is a passage describing David's sin with Bathsheba and its consequences (2 Sam 11–12), as well as a long section on the struggle of Absalom, and possibly others, for succession to the throne (chaps. 13–20). The purpose of the account in Samuel seems to be to establish Solomon as the legitimate heir, an eventuality never questioned by the Chronicler. Unique to the latter, however, is a chapter outlining details for the proposed temple (chap. 22), and a long passage listing David's royal and Levitical officials at the time the kingdom was handed over to Solomon (chaps. 23 – 29).

Details such as these form the basis for a literary-critical analysis. It is immediately evident that we are dealing with sources here, but each combined narrative is a skillful literary theological composition. In Samuel, particularly toward the end, the overwhelming interest is in the succession. We can therefore imagine that the narrative, or at least its sources, reflects a time when questions of dynastic legitimacy had not yet been settled. The earliest days of the monarchy best reflect these conditions, though the editing and compiling of the material perhaps took place later. Chronicles, by contrast, shows an overwhelming interest in the temple and its structure. From other evidence (2 Chr 36), we know that the final stage of the book came from the period after the Exile, so we must look for circumstances in the postexilic period which might illuminate a preoccupation with cult and temple. A study of Ezra-Nehemiah and the prophets Haggai and Zechariah gives the broad clue: Chronicles is a history of Israel written from the perspective of, or by the functionaries in, the rebuilt temple in Jerusalem.

A second type of doublet is also utilized by the literary critic. Here the question of pentateuchal sources becomes more relevant, and the study is more complex. For example, in Gen 12, 20, and 26 we find three accounts of what appear to be different events: in chap. 12, the king of Egypt takes Abraham's wife Sarai as a harem girl because Abraham said she was his sister; in chap. 20, Abimelech, the Philistine king of Gerar in the Negev, does the same thing, again because Abraham said she was his sister; in chap. 26, Abraham's son Isaac is in Gerar, and similarly tells Abimelech that his wife Rebekah is his sister. While Habel tends to view this general phenomenon in the Pentateuch as parallel accounts of the same tradition (he does not specifically treat the example outlined above), he warns that "it is not sufficient to grant the possibility of duplicate accounts based on the analogy of Samuel-Kings and Chronicles. We must also discern where the varying accounts begin and end."[20] Let us analyze the three accounts to see what we may find.

Applying first the criterion of divine names, we find that Gen 20 uses Elohim (except in v. 18), while chaps. 12 and 26 (except in v. 24) employ Yahweh. But is it clear that (1) the three accounts are best taken as variants of the same tradition, and (2) the three accounts can be related to different pentateuchal sources? Following the method we have outlined for a valid literary criticism, we find first that the internal structure or arrangement of all these accounts is the same. The details of person and place vary, of course, and chaps. 20 and 26 expand the story considerably over the shorter account of 12:10-20. But the literary type (here narrative, possibly of the saga variety) is common to all three. The themes of all are likewise similar and each account can be called a complete literary unit, although the context of each story determines part of its role.

What of stylistic features? Although older source critics were confident that they could distinguish between the Yahwist and the Elohist in these and similar narratives on stylistic grounds,[21] the major criterion remained that of the divine names. More recent critical analysis has shifted from an attempt to separate underlying documents on the basis of style (a difficult enterprise, unless the material varies to the extent of that in Gen 1 and 2), and turns instead to study the problem of how a single tradition could have developed into three accounts. This movement, which rightly stresses the similarity of the narratives, is nevertheless faced with the difficult task of differentiating between styles where little or no diversity may be discerned.

We have established by literary analysis that these are three very similar accounts, each purporting to represent a separate event in the patriarchal history. Internal structure and stylistic features follow a standardized pattern. But does it follow that there was only one original event? A. H. Sayce acknowledges that "doubtless history repeats itself; disputes about the possession of wells in a desert-land can frequently recur, and it is possible that two kings of the same name may have followed one another on

20. Habel, *Literary Criticism*, p. 10.
21. See Driver (*Genesis*, pp. xi-xvi) for criteria, and a remark that "the criteria 'istinguishing J from E are fewer and less clearly marked . . . ; and there is ⹁onsequently sometimes uncertainty in the analysis, and critics, interpreting the evidence differently, sometimes differ accordingly in their conclusions" (p. xii).

the throne of Gerar."[22] But at the same time, he expresses doubt that such details as the name Phicol could have been repeated. In the final analysis, the question is one of independent judgment. There are no canons by which such matters are proven, and at this point the interpreter with an evangelical view of Scripture will trust the text over his own feelings, one way or the other. The point I would like to stress is this: literary analysis has not been able, and cannot, prejudge the question of historicity. The above example could be extended to study a host of alleged doublets in the OT, but this one will illustrate the point.

A third type of so-called doublet occurs where two or more original accounts are apparently combined into one. We have already looked at one example in the study of divine names in Gen 6–9 (the deluge story). The source critic contends that by literary analysis he is able to discern and separate two parallel sources, and produce two reasonably self-contained versions of the story. The latter product is, in fact, what source analysts usually mean by "doublets." But is the method true to the best literary analysis? Is it not better to begin by assuming a unified composition, and ask whether the repetitions might not be best accounted for as a stylistic literary device by an ancient storyteller? O. T. Allis notes that

> (1) The repetitions are not meaningless. They bear directly upon the great emphases which have been pointed out . . . , and (2) the repetitions do not appear in every part of the narrative. There is only one account of the size of the ark (6:14-16), the sending out of the birds (8:6-12), the offering of sacrifice (8:20-21), the command regarding shedding blood and eating with the blood (9:36), the bow of promise (9:12-16).[23]

In fact, as noted in the analysis of Gen 7:16, there are places where only the finished form of the narrative makes sense of the parts. A true literary analysis will show that the final shape of Gen 6–9, with all its repetitions, does have an integrity of its own. It will seek to study the repetitions as they relate to thematic

22. A. H. Sayce, *The Early History of the Hebrews* (London: Rivingtons, 1897), p. 64 (quoted in Driver, *Genesis*, p. 254).

23. Allis, *Five Books of Moses*, p. 98.

development within the narrative, rather than impose a scheme which unnecessarily fractures the present text.

The study of doublets provides a very basic tool of our literary criticism, but analysis of the doublets must work with the established framework of the text. Plans which may be foreign to the literature under discussion must be avoided, for the critic seeks to isolate natural literary units, and then to study their style, structure, themes, and role in the larger whole. Along the way, he may find many clues to the background and dating of a given literary work, but these must come from within the text itself.

Differences in Detail

Conventional source criticism often separates sources on the basis of true or alleged discrepancies which may be observed in accounts of the same event or concept. As a literary criterion this method is limited, for a great deal of research into the factual basis of the OT should first be carried out by historians using the methods of historical criticism. But when, for example, we find two accounts of how to build an altar, neither of which seems aware of the other, as that in Exod 20:24-26 compared with the more sophisticated altars described in 27:1-8 (burnt offering) and 30:1-5 (incense), there are literary questions involved. While only the historian can illuminate the background for altars in early Israel, the literary critic must examine the literary context of each account.

In the cases we have cited, settings for the three passages on altars present themselves as highly distinctive. Exod 20:24-26, which speaks of simple altars of earth and unhewn stone, appears to be part of a very old collection of laws regulating personal and societal conduct in the land (Exod 20:22–23:19). While it contains legal material of various forms, the emphasis is on popular, lay-oriented activity. The final collection is probably the Book of the Covenant of Exod 24:7; this book is there read publicly at a ceremony of covenant ratification.

Exod 27 and 30, by contrast, occur in a portion of the book recording the directions which Yahweh gives regarding the priestly tabernacle, its furnishings, and its service (chaps. 25–31). In both form and content, the literary unit differs markedly from the Book of the Covenant, and this fact points to the reason for the difference in perspective of each. It is only by isolating the literary units by means of the dual criteria of structure and style that we understand the separate roles of the altars in question. The altars of Exod 20 relate to the common people, and are covered in the Covenant Code of popular law. The priestly altars of Exod 27 and 30 are related to the formal cultic structure of Israel's worship, and are described within a large block of priestly material. It is true that dating these blocks presents a further problem, but there is little reason to conclude that the core of either of them could not have originated at Sinai.

While examples could be multiplied, the preceding might serve to illustrate that even the conservative is dependent upon literary analysis to understand and explain divergence in such details. All problems will not be solved in this manner, of course, but studying the varieties of literature will greatly aid in elucidating each unit in turn. Comprehensive literary studies of subjects like ancient law add immeasurably to our understanding of legal texts, and the study of cultic forms similarly illuminates their context. The units reviewed above each have their setting in a separate life-situation, and they relate to different aspects of Israel's national life. Again, the matter of source documents has not been raised. Dividing the material into J, E, D, and P is of little help in this case, especially since these designations often connote outmoded views on the development of Israel's history and religion.

Theological Viewpoint

The publication in 1957 of Gerhard von Rad's first volume of *Theologie des Alten Testaments*[24] brought a Copernican revolution in OT studies. Whereas it was previously normal to speak of "*the* theology of the OT," it now became fashionable to speak in the plural of "OT theologies." Although von Rad by no means tied his theological conclusions to the classical documentary hypothesis, his work reflected a commonly held view that the documentary traditions speak in a variety of theological accents. Furthermore, the observation of this variant theological outlook

---

24. Gerhard von Rad, *Theologie des Alten Testaments*, vol. 1, *Die Theologie der historischen Überlieferungen Israels* (Munich: Christian Kaiser Verlag, 1957); Eng. trans. *Old Testament Theology*, vol. 1, *The Theology of Israel's Historical Traditions*, trans. D. M. G. Stalker (1962; reprint ed., London: SCM Press, 1975).

has for years been one of the pillars of source criticism. On the other hand, conservatives, who were concerned to maintain a unity of the biblical witness, have resisted this trend toward variety, though often at the cost of making Abraham, Moses, Amos, and Malachi all sound like an echo of St. Paul. Neither extreme has been helpful. There is within Scripture a great unity within its diversity, and literary analysis can help to discover both elements. Let us consider a few examples.

Gen 1 and 2 clearly represent two literary sources, and contribute different aspects to our total understanding of the God of creation. They present no conflict, however, for both Jews and Christians have always held that God is both transcendent (Gen 1) and immanent (Gen 2). Again, 2 Sam 7 and 1 Chr 17, both of which report the covenant given to David through the prophet Nathan, exhibit varied emphases, and a comparison between 2 Sam 7:16 and 1 Chr 17:14 illustrates the difference. "Your house and your kingdom shall be made sure" is a reflection of Samuel-Kings' political royal theology: the concern is God's coming messianic King. Chronicles reads, "But I will confirm him in my house and in my kingdom," a clear evidence of the interest in temple theology in the Chronicler's account. Here again there is no contradiction; as in the case of variants among the Synoptic Gospels, two texts which give essentially the same account are seen to serve each writer's inspired theological purposes.

Or yet again, consider a proposed contradiction between the theology of Exod 34:6-7, which teaches a collective guilt passing from generation to generation, and that of Deut 24:16; Jer 31:29-30; and Ezek 18:4, 20, all of which present a doctrine of individual responsibility. This phenomenon is frequently explained by employing a developmental view of Israel's religion. Exod 34:6-7 is assigned to J, a reflection of the collective covenant theology of the early monarchy under David. Deut 24, which on this view is dated to 621 B.C., is seen as antithetical, that is, as a reaction against the harsh collectivism of the earlier period, while Jer 31:30 and Ezek 18:3 explicitly repudiate the old proverb which says, "The fathers have eaten sour grapes, and the children's teeth are set on edge." Setting aside for the moment the documentary hypothesis, let us see how literary criticism might otherwise approach the question. Examination of the literary and historical context of each passage would seem a reasonable place to begin.

The Exodus passage occurs in the context of God's self-revelation in the Sinai covenant, and the larger literary unit which relates the event (Exod 32–34) stresses this side of God's holy activity. By contrast, Jeremiah and Ezekiel represent a very different historical and theological context, though each differs again from the other. The quotation from Jeremiah occurs in his so-called Book of Consolation, a picture of life under the New Covenant, while Ezekiel cites the proverb to repudiate the old order which passed away at the Exile.

But what of Deuteronomy? Does not its similarity to the later prophets prove the lateness of the literary unit? Again, we must examine the purpose and intent of the passage. Deut 12–26 contains varied instructions for the people of Israel in the land, not unlike the material found in the Book of the Covenant in Exodus. Deut 24:16, in this context, far from constituting an early (or late) contradiction of Exod 34:6-7, sets out the judicial procedure to be followed in Israel when an individual is found guilty of the breach of specific civil enactments or case law precedents. The collective guilt of a broken covenant may continue, but judicial procedure does not hold families guilty for individual crimes.

Thus a basic literary analysis of each passage in question clarifies and resolves what originally appears to present a contradiction. No recourse to source theories is in this case required; the historical, theological, and literary context of the literary units provides a reasonable basis for accepting the integrity of each.

Style

Certain stylistic features have already been examined in our study of Gen 1–4,[25] but only with reference to the way structure and subject matter affect vocabulary. The classical view of literary or source analysis went further, and proposed for each of the underlying documents of the OT a distinctive vocabulary which could be determined by analysis and then used as a criterion for additional separation of sources in the remainder of the OT. Earlier source critics were more confident in this enterprise, and lists of J, E, D, and P words or expressions were regularly cited.[26] But from the beginning it was generally acknowledged that the method applied more readily to a separation between P and JE,[27] where

25. In the section above on method.
26. E.g., Driver, *Genesis,* pp. vii-xi (P), and p. xii (J and E).
27. Ibid., p. xii.

distinctives were determined on the basis of subject matter and form rather than on the special vocabulary of a particular writer. We have seen how easily separate units may be discerned in Gen 1 and 2; the principles involved may be extended to Gen 5, a genealogy of the line from Adam through Seth to Noah. Gen 5:1-3 quite clearly draws on terminology from Gen 1:26-28, and the chapter generally uses the divine name Elohim, except for v. 29 which reflects the narrative section from Gen 3:17-19. The rest of the chapter is similar to Gen 1 only in that it follows a "stereotyped form";[28] it exhibits no distinctive vocabulary as such. A comparison with the genealogy of Gen 4:17-26, however, will show that the expression "he became the father of" (Hebrew hiphil *wayyôled*; *KJV* "he begat") consistently recurs in Gen 5 but is absent from Gen 4:17-26. The latter employs various expressions in describing birth, all of which are different from the recurrent pattern of Gen 5. Again, it would seem plausible to posit two separate literary units, but the basis for this supposition would be the internal structure and overall coherence rather than specific vocabulary alone.

Actually, there is very little to go on in these chapters, and what is given is too often ambiguous. Gen 4:17-26 carries the two lines of Cain and Seth to separate climaxes, while 5:1-32 picks up the Seth line and provides a genealogical transition to Noah. Gen 4:17-26, which uses the name Yahweh (except in direct speech by Eve, v. 25), has no distinctive birth formula and follows the more narrative style of chaps. 2–4. Gen 5:1-3 builds on 1:26-28, while 5:28-31 (the Lamech genealogy, in form like the rest of chap. 5) is related to Gen 3:17-19. Elohim is generally used (except in v. 29, which is direct speech by Lamech), and a certain formula or pattern recurs. These data provide hardly enough evidence to link either chapter to a documentary hypothesis, but they do, on other grounds, point to separate literary or formal units. In fact, the formula in Gen 5:1, "This is the book of the generations of Adam," is also found in 2:4; 6:9; and 10:1, and would seem to mark off separate literary units, at least if the colophon always comes at the beginning of each section rather than at the end. In this case, of course, we should have to view Gen 2:4a as relating to chaps. 2–4 rather than to the "P" section preceding.

28. Ibid., p. 74.

We conclude that distinctive vocabulary is sometimes less than certain as a criterion for dividing the Pentateuch, and that the method may even produce notable inconsistencies.[29] Yet the criterion may be applied with a measure of consistency, for example, to Gen 4 and 5, and the fact remains that despite certain excesses in the past, it is often possible to discover unique features of style in a particular literary unit. The conservative critic, for example, can readily discern distinct vocabulary preferences between Hosea and Amos, two contemporary northern prophets. But in this case separate authorship is a known fact. Between Gen 4:17-26 and 5:1-32, or between Exodus and Deuteronomy, the matter is more complicated. Many observable differences relate to subject matter (e.g., Deuteronomy is a restatement of God's covenant, and therefore reflects covenant terminology), while others may reflect the form of an original unit (e.g., the formal genealogical patterns of Gen 5). If the criterion of standardized vocabulary could be applied with more consistent results, it might commend itself as a canon for dividing the entire Pentateuch. Even true to its own presuppositions, however, the scheme produces so many problems that many critics have abandoned it altogether.

By contrast, a more viable literary criticism can still use the criteria of style and vocabulary in, for example, the book of Deuteronomy. But without limitation to a developmental hypothesis about how the religion and history of Israel unfolded, other questions may be asked as to the origin of forms present in the book. Answers to these questions can often be found without unnecessarily doubting the integrity of the material as we have received it, or importing an alien and subjective methodology to the study.

Summary

We have tried to show that the methods used by literary critics, though basically sound, have suffered from a serious overextension of their validity when tied to a theory of documentary sources that follows any preconceived developmental scheme for Israel's history or literature. This criticism is certainly acknowledged by many modern literary critics,[30] and it forms the basis of a great

---

29. See Allis, *Five Books of Moses*, pp. 40-59, 60-78.
30. E.g., Habel, *Literary Criticism*, p. 41 n. 8.

deal of form-critical attack on source analysis.[31] At the same time, many source critics still hold that the accumulated weight of stylistic data leads to the inescapable conclusion that three (JE, D, and P), four (J, E, D, and P), or more dated literary sources may be discerned in the Pentateuch. Habel, it is true, holds that "these hypotheses are secondary" to the other new insights which may be gained through literary criticism,[32] but he still devotes 66 of his 84 pages to these views. I wish to suggest that the evidence clearly warrants a separation of blocks of material, but does not point to four unified sources.

CONCLUSION

The OT scholar must, on account of the nature of the material he studies, be also a literary critic. The inspired Word has come to us in "many and various ways" (*polymerôs kaì polytrópōs*), and the OT is especially rich in literary variety. In many cases, the writings with which we are concerned are undated and anonymous, and in other instances they reflect obvious use of varied sources or units by the inspired author. Our task, while avoiding subjective schemas, is to use all the tools of the true literary critic to appreciate more fully the background, the forms, the development of thought, and the role of each unit in its context. To ignore these tools would be folly, and conservative scholarship has never really done so, as a study of the works of critics from Calvin to the present will bear witness. Let us not be afraid of the term "criticism." Rather, let us blend scholarship and respect for God's Holy Word into a new and vital force for understanding and communicating the divine revelation.

31. See especially some of the criticism from Scandinavia, e.g., Ivan Engnell, *A Rigid Scrutiny: Critical Essays on the Old Testament*, trans. John T. Willis (Nashville: Vanderbilt University Press, 1969).
32. Habel, *Literary Criticism*, p. 84.

III
Form Criticism

INTRODUCTION

In the years since 1900, a new branch of biblical criticism has arisen which, since the publication in 1919 of Martin Dibelius's *Die Formgeschichte des Evangeliums* (the form history of the Gospels),[1] has been known as form criticism. In OT research the discipline was established at the turn of the century by the pioneering work of Hermann Gunkel, whose study of literary forms or types in both Genesis and Psalms set an example for future generations.[2] In the years since the Second World War, form-critical research, and the twin studies of tradition history and oral tradition, have come to dominate OT studies, beginning on the continent and spreading to England and North America.

Definition

For the average reader, form criticism is far more difficult to define and comprehend than straightforward source or literary criticism. To some form critics, the subject seems to encompass the critical enterprise from beginning to end,[3] but in attempting

1. Martin Dibelius, *Die Formgeschichte des Evangeliums* (Tübingen: J. C. B. Mohr, 1919); Eng. trans. of 2d Ger. ed., *From Tradition to Gospel*, trans. Bertram Lee Woolf (New York: Charles Scribner's Sons, 1935).
2. E.g., Hermann Gunkel, *The Legends of Genesis*, trans. W. H. Carruth (New York: Schocken Books, Schocken Paperback ed., 1964), which first appeared as the introduction to his commentary on Genesis (Göttingen: Vandenhoeck & Ruprecht, 1901); idem, *The Psalms: A Form-Critical Introduction*, trans. Thomas M. Horner, Facet Books, Biblical Series 19 (Philadelphia: Fortress Press, 1967), from his article on the Psalms in the 2d ed. of *Religion in Geschichte und Gegenwart*, 5 vols. (Tübingen: J. C. B. Mohr, 1927-31), 4:1609-27.
3. E.g., Klaus Koch, *The Growth of the Biblical Tradition: The Form-Critical Method*, trans. S. M. Cupitt from 2d Ger. ed. (London: Adam & Charles Black, 1969).

43

to define it we shall look for the features which distinguish it from related disciplines. What then is form criticism, or "type criticism" (*Gattungsgeschichte*) as Gunkel called it? Is it compatible with evangelical views of revelation and inspiration? Klaus Koch defines it as "an attempt to discover the principles underlying the language of the Bible." But he is careful to add that "this does not and must not imply a mere structural and generic linguistic study."[4] In other words, a form critic studies not merely the sentence as a unit of human speech, but the literary types of speech. It is the discovery of the sociological role or function of each type in its original setting that is the goal of form-critical work.

In a student handbook titled *Form Criticism of the Old Testament*, Gene M. Tucker puts it another way. Stressing the commonality of literary or spoken genres to all societies, Tucker sees form criticism as "a method of analyzing and interpreting the literature of the Old Testament through a study of its literary types or genres."[5] An important addition to the previous statement will help to clarify the definition. Tucker stresses that the real distinctive of form-critical work is its concern with the oral stage or preliterary aspect of the writings.[6] Here is the point at which form criticism divides from literary criticism. While literary criticism is concerned with the development of written or literary sources, form criticism by definition attempts to reconstruct the history of the saying or unit in its prewritten forms. Two assumptions are implicit in these propositions: (1) every written document was preceded by some oral stage of development; and (2) something can be learned of the oral stage or stages by a study of analogous literary forms. A third assumption is equally important, namely, that a history of the preliterary stages of a given work will shed light on the finished literary product. Each of these needs to be tested against the methods employed and against the results claimed by form-critical research, and we will examine each in turn.

Origin

In a certain sense, the rise of form criticism implied that source

4. Ibid., p. xiii.
5. Gene M. Tucker, *Form Criticism of the Old Testament*, Guides to Biblical Scholarship, Old Testament Series (Philadelphia: Fortress Press, 1971), p. 1.
6. Ibid.

criticism was inadequate to write a literary history of the OT corpus. The assumption that various hands could be discovered and classified within the books of Scripture left open too many questions. Both substantial similarities in style or expression and also distinctive differences could be observed upon comparing many texts, and these could not all be explained on the basis of literary dependence. Furthermore, the evolutionary approach of older source criticism failed to account for the obvious antiquity of certain material within the putative sources. A study of ancient Near Eastern literature was sufficient to convince scholars like Gunkel, his associate Hugo Gressmann, and Gunkel's pupil Sigmund Mowinckel that the key to understanding the literature lay not in dividing the text into documents but in the forms of traditional speech which lay behind the later compositions.

Ignoring attacks on source criticism by traditional conservatives like Keil and Hengstenberg, but open to the idea of a much greater antiquity for portions of the OT, these men looked to the surrounding cultures and their literature for solutions to OT problems. They felt that the key to understanding a given prophetic oracle, an Israelite law, or a hymn to Yahweh lay in its similarity to analogous forms from the world around Israel. They soon developed a concomitant view that these forms, which grew out of the life of the community and were often quite stereotyped, had a long and complicated history of oral development and transmission. Applying these principles to Israel's literature, they developed the study of literary "type" (Gunkel's *Gattung*), or, as it came to be called, "form history" (*Formgeschichte*).

Though originally something of a protest movement against source criticism, it is important to note that contemporary form critics usually affirm a chastened and modified source theory as the second stage in the task of OT research.[7] Most of them also share the naturalistic presuppositions of the "liberal" view of revelation — or indeed of no view of revelation — mentioned in Chapter I above. It is important, then, before proceeding, to ask in what way or ways an evangelical understanding of revelation and inspiration might affect our response to the subject.

Relation to Revelation

As we have already observed, an evangelical doctrine of inspi-

---

7. E.g., J. C. Rylaarsdam, Foreword to Tucker, *Form Criticism*, pp. vi-vii; von Rad, *Genesis*, pp. 24-31.

ration and revelation leaves open many questions of authorship, dating, and source. But in contrast to other views, an evangelical holds that the final product of the process may be read with confidence as the Word of God. That is to say, with a proper understanding of the hermeneutical (interpretative) issues involved a Christian may expect to hear God speaking directly and infallibly in the very words of prophets and apostles. He will also expect that when the pages of Scripture assert a fact as true or describe an event as having happened, that fact will be true and that event will have happened. This is, I believe, where a certain line must be drawn.[8]

It is not always clear, however, that a given scripture is truly asserting what we may on the surface take as its meaning. As a basic historical example I take the chronological framework of the book of Judges. In the early period, that is, the period of the first four good judges (Othniel, Ehud, Deborah/Barak, and Gideon), three of the four cycles close with the stereotyped expression "So the land had rest [*wattišqōṭ*] forty years" (3:11; 5:31; 8:28), while the fourth uses the same expression but doubles the number to eighty (3:30). It would be highly unusual (though not impossible) for each of these judges to have had identical regnal periods, and the presence of a stereotyped formula suggests that the expression may not be intended to express an exact chronology. It appears to be telling us, rather, that in this early era the results of God's work through His servants was a long period (generation?) of rest. This is not a question about the fallibility of Scripture, but rather a question about what the Bible intends us to believe.

Here is the basic line beyond which an evangelical, in the tradition of the Protestant Reformers and great defenders of the faith like C. F. Keil, B. B. Warfield, and Robert Dick Wilson, cannot go. The Word of God is truth in all that it asserts to be true. But how does this influence our response to questions of oral tradition, of formal and stylistic development, of theories of linguistic pattern? These are questions we must answer in the context of a theological commitment.

As has been clearly demonstrated in NT studies, there was a

8. See also John Goldingay, "Inspiration, Infallibility, and Criticism," *The Churchman* 90 (1976):20.

period of oral transmission of the Gospel accounts.[9] Indeed, Paul can affirm the truth-value of the death, burial, and resurrection of Christ precisely because he "received" (*paralambánō*) the tradition on good authority (1 Cor 15:3-7). The truth of the event, and its saving significance, was in no way affected by the fact that it was not communicated in writing in the first instance. The Lukan prologue (1:2) can use the same word (*paradídomi*) employed by Paul in 1 Cor 15:3, and speak of those traditions "delivered" by eyewitnesses and servants of the Word, presumably by a person-to-person process. Again, the truth-value is not affected by the nature of the transmission. True, evangelical NT critics have welcomed recent studies which argue for an earlier commitment to written form,[10] but they have never accepted the form-critical argument that increasing error is a corollary to a longer period of oral transmission. Even the fact that each Evangelist was a creative theologian, casting his material in a framework designed to stress one or more great aspects of our Lord's ministry or person, has never been seen as affecting the truth content of the Gospel narratives. While studying the ways in which each Evangelist used the traditions received, we can still have confidence that the Holy Spirit has given us accurate, trustworthy accounts of the person and work of the Lord from heaven.

In the OT the same combination of factors can be applied. It must be immediately apparent that the material in Gen 1 – 11 was handed down from person to person and carried by patriarchal bards (possibly in the form of poetic epic) from Mesopotamia to Canaan, to Egypt, and back again. In addition, there can be little question that the forms of creation stories (cosmogonies and cosmologies) were fairly stereotyped in the mythologies of the world out of which Abraham was called. Josh 24:2 reminds us that the patriarchs came from a pagan environment, a milieu which we might expect to find reflected in their creation theology. That the form of their cosmogonies is similar to those of the ancient world, while the content is dissimilar, leads to the probable conclusion that their orally transmitted mythologies provided the formal or structural basis for the Genesis accounts,

9. See George Eldon Ladd, *The New Testament and Criticism* (Grand Rapids: Wm. B. Eerdmans, 1967), pp. 148-50.
10. E.g., John A. T. Robinson, *Redating the New Testament* (Philadelphia: Westminster Press, 1976).

while the theological content displayed a new understanding received by revelation.

The case of creation narratives is not unique. In many other parts of the OT we find passages whose form reflects standard literary patterns and whose content is uniquely Israelite. In some instances (e.g., the legal codes of Exodus and Numbers), both oral and written sources can be objectively verified from the ancient Near East. In other cases (e.g., narrative traditions recorded in the historical works), there is no direct evidence for oral transmission, and we must be careful to avoid false applications of the method. In any case, many of these are questions of historical and literary debate[11] and not matters of theological substance.

This is not to say, however, that evangelicals will be comfortable with all modern form-critical methods or conclusions. A critique on literary grounds will be offered later, but at this point I would like to suggest two foci at which an evangelical theology of revelation and inspiration conflicts with current form-critical tendencies.

Classification of forms. First, many form critics hold an unduly skeptical view of supernatural elements in Scripture. Certain phenomena described in the OT (e.g., the miracle at the Red Sea) are classified as embellishments of folk tradition largely because the critic does not believe in direct divine intervention in human affairs. Here again the basic criterion in classifying a form must be derived from induction. How does the biblical record intend the account to be taken? If it could be shown that, for example, Gen 1–11 was intended as "myth" (a difficult term to define), then the evangelical critic should have no objection to the classification. Or again, if the book of Jonah was intended as an allegory, then that is how an evangelical would want to take it. But too often the narrative gives no hint of such an intention; the category is created and applied by the critic on the basis of his lack of sympathy for the categories of divine revelation. Thus, for example, the story of Balaam's ass in Num 22 becomes a folktale or a fable rather than history, though apart from the appearance

---

11. Cf. K. A. Kitchen, *Ancient Orient and Old Testament* (Chicago: Inter-Varsity Press, 1966), pp. 135-38.

of the angel and the speech of the ass the account bears no marks of a fable.

Determination of origins. Second, form criticism often assumes a non-Israelite origin for a particular account or tradition simply because the narrative shows formal similarities to a pagan model. The objection is not to finding the formal similarities, but to the conclusion that Israel's traditions can be explained or explained away because of the manner in which they are recounted. This method is particularly questionable when the *Sitz im Leben* or life-setting of a given tradition is clearly stated in the text (e.g., the main features of the Joseph story), but another life-setting is created in its place.

METHOD

All form critics employ certain steps in their method, though the procedure to be followed after the last step would not be called form criticism by all practitioners of the discipline. The steps are four: (1) analyze the structure of a given passage to define the literary or form-critical unit; (2) describe the genre, type, or form; (3) look for a *Sitz im Leben* or life-setting for the genre in general; and (4) determine the function or purpose of the unit by means of comparison with the history of that genre. Let us examine each in turn.

Define the Unit

Since the purpose of form criticism is to study the preliterary history of individual units, it is of paramount importance to determine the extent of each. Often this extent is self-evident, as for example with a psalm like Ps 1, or a short prophetic oracle like Amos 5:1-17 (though sections within the latter unit have been questioned). On other occasions, both in poetry and narrative, the question is more complicated. Ps 19, for example, changes subject matter at v. 7 and appears originally to have been two units; the first six verses deal with creation and the last eight with the law. But subject matter is not the only determining factor — there should be formal literary distinctives as well. As we shall see, students of hymnic literature have found these, and the original units are in fact quite easy to trace.

Klaus Koch tackles a more difficult question in attempting to separate individual units from a continuous narrative.[12] Using criteria like the observation of an introductory formula $way^eh\hat{\imath}$ (*KJV* "And it came to pass . . ."), Koch finds originally separate units in Gen 12:10-20; 20:1-17; and 26:1-13. To render the method plausible, there must also be evidence that these units sit loosely in their present literary context, and this Koch attempts to show for each of the three narratives. Whether the evidence is convincing must remain an open question, but it must be admitted that this is one of the more subjective foundations of the form-critical endeavor. Where units are clearly separate, or where subject matter as well as form signals a break, the task is easier. In a connected narrative, however, there are bound to be changes in subject matter, and the forms adduced to signal a new unit are often the standard transitional phrases by which a narrative moves from one incident to the next. Koch's view that these narrative units differ from others in the Abraham cycle is based on the observation that they are not required to round out a continuous chronological sequence. For that reason it is certainly not impossible to think of them as insertions placed, like many other narratives, out of chronological order. But to suggest that they were originally separate in a form-critical sense requires more careful judgment.

Describe the Genre

On the assumption that clear and separate units have been distinguished, the next step is to determine their literary types "irrespective of their present, written context."[13] The last phrase is an important reminder that, for the form critic, it is not the present but the original context which determines meaning.

Again, the text must provide the clues, although a knowledge of contemporary literary forms will provide the criteria for making decisions. In the example cited from the Psalms, there is little question that Ps 19 is lyric poetry of the category called "hymns." The first six verses, moreover, are an old hymn of praise to God in creation.[14] These verses must be studied first (but not only)

---

12. Koch, *Growth of Biblical Tradition*, pp. 111-18.
13. Ibid., p. 119.
14. Sigmund Mowinckel, *The Psalms in Israel's Worship*, trans. D. R. Ap-Thomas, 2 vols. (New York: Abingdon Press, 1962), 1:90-91.

in comparison with creation hymns, both within the OT and in the wider ancient Near East. But vv. 7-14 constitute what Sigmund Mowinckel has called a "hymn to the Law of the Lord."[15] The interpreter would later want to ask the very basic question of why these two hymns have been juxtaposed, and the answer would provide a key to the present meaning of the psalm. As a prior step, however, he must know something about the categories originally used in each component part.

Regarding the more complex question of narrative, we note that the example of the Abraham cycle cited above is classed by Gunkel among the "poetic narratives," a term signifying prose which aims "to please, to elevate, to inspire, and to move,"[16] rather than simply to inform. The many categories of narrative, sometimes quite baldly transferred from western folklore to the biblical setting, have been variously catalogued as myth, folktale, saga, legend, fable, and novelette.[17] Over against poetic prose are set history and the various materials of which history is constructed (chronicles, annals, contracts, letters, genealogies, memoirs, etc.). Koch follows Gunkel in calling the narratives in Gen 12, 20, and 26 "sagas" (rather than the misleading Eng. trans. "legends"),[18] a genre which presents prehistoric historiography in a traditional or popular form. Neither Gunkel nor his successors intended to prejudge the question of whether the events portrayed in saga actually occurred, though most have argued for a process of continuous fictional accretion as the stories developed.

If the terms usually employed to designate prehistorical narrative are found objectionable, the evangelical critic might seek fresh terminology. But by standard definitions, history requires the presence of written records; thus the history of Israel prior to Moses is not, strictly speaking, presented in historical form. Again, the key to our understanding must be provided by the

15. Ibid., p. 90.

16. Gunkel, *Legends of Genesis*, pp. 10, 11.

17. For lists see, e.g., Gunkel, *Legends of Genesis*, chaps. 1 – 2; Tucker, *Form Criticism*, pp. 26-41; various OT introductions, including Eissfeldt, *The Old Testament: An Introduction*; J. Alberto Soggin, *Introduction to the Old Testament*, trans. John Bowden, Old Testament Library (Philadelphia: Westminster Press, 1976); Artur Weiser, *Introduction to the Old Testament*, trans. Dorothea M. Barton (London: Darton, Longman & Todd, 1961).

18. Koch, *Growth of Biblical Tradition*, pp. 118-19; cf. the comments of W. F. Albright, Introduction to Gunkel, *Legends of Genesis*, pp. xi-xii.

materials themselves. G. H. Livingston has made an impressive attempt to articulate these literary forms in the context of Israelite thought. He suggests a variety of types, and links the three narratives mentioned above to a covenant framework plus man's response to that covenant. He finds in Gen 12, 20, and 26 several examples of what he has named a Moral Violation of the Covenant type, a genre which he discerns throughout the Pentateuch.[19] The study of ancient literary genres has only begun. In principle the investigation is both valid and necessary, and evangelicals should not ignore the work that has been done. Hopefully the evangelical critic will be able to contribute to a continuing search for valid criteria by which to catalogue the genre of the units. The major problems lie in the study of narrative types, while poetic and prophetic speech forms more readily lend themselves to such analysis.

Determine the Life-Setting

Although Koch argues at this point for a need to trace transmission history in order to move backward to the life-setting,[20] the enterprise is regarded by many as a separate discipline. Tucker is more representative of form critics in general in affirming that one can directly derive the setting from the genre. The setting, as Tucker notes, is not primarily a reference to the date or historical period of a genre, but rather to the sociological context (e.g., cultic, legal, political) from which the unit of tradition arose.[21] Thus, not only in the case of hymnic literature but often with legal or narrative material as well, the context is worship, whether communal worship or individual piety. In the case of wisdom sayings the setting is often the school, while for prophetic oracles the setting is usually one of proclamation.

At this stage I would like to comment on two problems which arise. The first comes from the tendency of form critics to study the smallest possible unit of tradition rather than an entire literary unit. For example, a prophetic formula like "Thus says the LORD" is rightly seen as reflecting the world of the royal herald or the call to order in a law court. But the critic should not be

---

19. G. H. Livingston, *The Pentateuch and Its Cultural Environment* (Grand Rapids: Baker Book House, 1974), pp. 241-60.
20. Koch, *Growth of Biblical Tradition*, pp. 112-27.
21. Tucker, *Form Criticism*, p. 15.

content with the fragmentation implied in breaking up the text into such small units. Meaning is derived ultimately from the life-setting in which these fragmentary traditional phrases or units were combined into a genre, the setting of which is integral to the whole. Thus, for example, Amos is not to be understood merely by analogy to the law court or the royal household, but in the context of the prophetic movement. That this movement in the eighth century B.C. drew on traditional forms of speech will help us to appreciate the form and content of the prophecy, but the life-setting of the whole is ultimately of more value than the life-setting of its parts.

A second problem relates to the desire of the form critic to work as far backward as he can in search of a setting. Of course, if the transmission history of a given unit were clear this would present no problems. For example, in tracing artistic or musical motifs, we often have their history clearly preserved in what we know of the connections between various artists or musicians. Thus, in the paintings of J. M. W. Turner (1775-1851) we can see the clear influence, both positive and negative, of Lorrain Claude (1600-1682), though the two represent different national origins and indeed widely separate periods. In the same way, W. A. Mozart (1756-1791) openly built on the work of G. F. Handel (1685-1759) in a manner not unfamiliar to students of music. But more to the point, all these artists also reflect long traditions of expression, of color, and of form, many of which were employed quite unconsciously. That we can trace these at all is possible primarily because we have a rather complete knowledge of art, architecture, and music in the periods both during and before each man produced his work. In OT literature, the critic is often working without this knowledge. Not only in questions of clear literary dependence but also in the more vexing problem of traditional forms and their settings there is often a paucity of data. We simply do not know enough about ancient literary forms to draw some of the conclusions on life-setting which have been proposed.

The evangelical critic does well to limit his assertions about life-setting to those which can be clearly derived from the context of the unit, or from obvious allusions in the language of the passage. Thus it may be a great help to relate the wisdom sayings to the schools of international wisdom, or worship forms to the cultic life of the nation. Even in the case of cosmology and cosmogony, we may trace the original form back to the mythology of the ancient Near East. But the final key to the meaning is to be found in the setting within Israel, for this is the place and the setting in which God was pleased to reveal Himself. In many and various ways God spoke, but since it was to the fathers through the prophets it was Israel who provided the final context or life-setting, whatever transmission history we can legitimately trace.

Determine the Function

Tucker carefully separates this step from what is called "redaction criticism." The form critic, as mentioned above, is concerned to discover the intention of the genre in its ancient setting.[22] The redaction critic, by contrast, would be concerned with the unit as it was used by the final collector or editor, who is referred to as a redactor. Let me illustrate by reference again to Ps 19 and the cycle of accounts in Gen 12, 20, and 26.

In Ps 19, the final redactor brought together a creation hymn and a hymn to the law of the Lord for a definite didactic purpose. The redaction critic seeks to discover the process of combination and the function of the final product. The form critic, in contrast, works with the component genres (i.e., the hymn to creation in vv. 1-6 and the hymn to law in vv. 7-14), asking what function or intention each might have served in its original setting.

The first part of the psalm may have had an original setting or life-situation quite outside of Israel, for the creation hymn is ubiquitous in the ancient Near East. The form critic might first ask: what function did the hymn serve when people were not monotheists and creation was seen in a mythological context? But even more to the point for an evangelical critic: is there any evidence that this particular creation hymn or its theology is compatible with ancient ideas of creation? As it stands now, one would hardly answer in the affirmative. The very fact that its majestic lines have provided Jewish and Christian poets with source material for celebrating creation bears witness to the distinctiveness of this creation hymn. But some form critics find pre-Israelite mythological forms in the psalm,[23] so they must at least

22. Ibid., pp. 16-17.
23. E.g., Mowinckel, *Psalms in Israel's Worship*, 2:267 n. XL.

ask questions about the intent of the creation hymn outside Israel. Most evangelical critics would not doubt the validity of this search, though they might question its relevance to exegesis and interpretation. It is at this level, after all, that form criticism claims to make its contribution.[24]

For the second part of the hymn, which is a different subgenre, the setting and intention of the original form are of greater value. Here the life-setting is clearly within the social or cultural world of Israel, and thus the intention of the original genre can be directly linked to the growth of Israelite piety. But the redactor's intent is ultimately more important than the intention of the genre in its original setting, for in the redactor's purpose its revelational content becomes normative.

Regarding the narratives in Gen 12, 20, and 26, Koch follows Gunkel in calling these "ethnological sagas," and finds also "a host of smaller component types."[25] But what is the intention of each ancient genre? Peeling away layers of traditional accretions, Koch reduces the original saga to a type of bedouin tale emphasizing the role of God in relation to a particular people, and explaining the subsequent relations among various nomadic or ethnic groups.[26] For Koch, the transmission history provides a vital link between original saga and final redaction, and the original setting or intention is only one of several settings or intentions through which the narrative passed. A cautious critic might question the objectivity of the method itself, but I would suggest a further critique from a theological perspective. Even if it could be shown that Koch's original life-setting was correct for ethnological sagas in general, is it possible to find in that setting any revelational intent or function? As a literary background it may, when objectively constructed, illuminate forms of Israelite communication, but the so-called ancient setting has little to do with the revelational function of the text of our present Bible.

This is not to question the method when the setting of the genre is clearly within the revelational framework of the sacred history; it is rather to suggest that the so-called original narrative genres from the ancient Near East at best provide a literary analogy and at worst may be substantially misleading. Is there

---

24. Tucker, *Form Criticism*, p. 17.
25. Koch, *Growth of Biblical Tradition*, p. 120.
26. Ibid., pp. 119-20, 120-28.

any evidence that the story was written to embody the motives of primitive ethnological saga? Is there any evidence that such an intention forms any basis for interpreting the account today? In the absence of relevant data, the evangelical critic should exercise caution.

FURTHER EXAMPLES OF AN EVANGELICAL FORM CRITICISM

Here are additional illustrations of how an evangelical might employ form-critical research in the service of his exegesis in the OT. Examples are taken from passages to which the method is particularly applicable, and which further serve to exhibit certain limits of that method. These are followed by a summary of the various limitations and strengths of the method for the evangelical critic.

Prose Genres

In OT prose narratives perhaps the greatest single advance during the past fifty years has been facilitated by the recovery of ancient Near Eastern covenant or treaty formulas. Julius Wellhausen was once of the opinion that the idea of a covenant "does not occur in the earlier prophets at all," and again, that "the idea of a covenant between Yahweh and Israel did not gain general significance until shortly before the Exile."[27] Wellhausen was not, of course, disputing an earlier use of the term *bĕrît* ("covenant, treaty"); it is the content of the word as a description of legal relationship between two contracting parties to which he assigned a later date. Wellhausen's theory is now obsolete in many respects, while the antiquity of Yahweh's covenant with Israel has more recently been argued in various quarters and on varied grounds.[28] Our present interest is the combined results of archeological evidence and form-critical research which have given a totally new understanding of the role of covenant, and illuminated the ancient background of many texts to which Wellhausen had given a later date.

---

27. Wellhausen, *Geschichte Israels* (Berlin: Georg Reimer, 1878), pp. 434-35 n. 1; quoted by Klaus Baltzer, *The Covenant Formulary*, trans. David E. Green (Oxford: Basil Blackwell, 1971), p. 1.
28. Baltzer, *Covenant Formulary*, pp. 6-8 and nn. 44-48.

In the years since 1920, a host of studies have shown that second-millennium Hittite treaties follow a particular formal structure,[29] and this structure was later discovered to be present in OT covenant narratives as well.[30] These covenants contain six standard elements, often in the same order: (1) an opening or preamble; (2) a historical prologue; (3) a statement concerning the future relationship of the contracting parties; (4) a list of stipulations; (5) an invocation of the deities as witnesses; and (6) a list of curses and blessings contingent upon the keeping or breaking of the contract. Some treaties combine the second and third elements, and some add provisions for depositing a copy in the sanctuary and for regular public reading,[31] but these minor variants do not disturb the basic pattern.

Form critics have been quick to seize on the similarities between ancient Near Eastern treaties and those of the OT, and Josh 24 provides a good working model of the relationship.[32] Six or seven elements of ancient covenant may be observed here in the same general order as those of the Hittites, and these provide the structure of the chapter.

Step one of the method outlined previously notes that Josh 24:1-27 forms a distinct unit containing a six- or sevenfold outline of covenantal elements. Step two attempts to determine the literary type, and again this is supplied by the parallel with the Hittite treaties. Here it should be stressed that the treaty form supplies only the type for the original formal unit; as the chapter stands, it is not so much a formal treaty as a word of exhortation forming part of Joshua's farewell speech to Israel. The third step determines a life-setting for the form or genre; here again the answer is provided by the analogy from comparative studies. It should be noted, however, that the analogy says nothing as to how the treaty form came to be used by Israel as a means of communicating God's covenant laws. Moreover, the true setting of chap. 24 is no longer treaty making in the ancient

29. Ibid., p. 9 n. 2.
30. G. E. Mendenhall, *Law and Covenant in Israel and the Ancient Near East* (Pittsburgh: Biblical Colloquium, 1955).
31. Kitchen, *Ancient Orient and Old Testament*, pp. 92-93.
32. It should be noted, however, that the thesis has not gone unchallenged. See, e.g., D. J. McCarthy, *Treaty and Covenant: A Study in Form in the Ancient Oriental Documents and in the Old Testament*, rev. ed. (Rome: Pontifical Biblical Institute, 1978), pp. 234-42.

world. It is, rather, the divine disclosure of a sovereign God to a people whom He has called out of Mesopotamian paganism and redeemed from bondage in Egypt.

Here again we are brought face to face with the question of what *Sitz im Leben* might actually be the key to understanding this unit. Certainly the treaty forms of the Hittite empire have provided a much greater awareness of the literary and legal aspects of Josh 24 and numerous other passages. But this life-situation is not in itself the setting of divine revelation; the latter came when God, using the forms of ancient treaties, entered into relationships with Abraham, Isaac, and Jacob. The subsequent giving of the law, also in treaty form, and its later affirmation in Josh 24, are themselves of a revelational character to which no ancient secular setting could ever do justice.

Step four ascertains the intent or function of the form. Again, with the ancient treaties, this is relatively simple. But here one must ask: what does this indicate about the intention or function of Josh 24? There can be little doubt that the parallel does tell something of God and His relationships to mankind, namely, that they are based on previous acts of mercy, are legally binding, and are dependent on mutual commitments. But function goes much deeper than mere form. The intent of Josh 24 in its current setting is the key to its meaning, and to find this intention the form critic must be able to assume the role of redaction critic or canon critic as well.

It will be seen how form criticism can help one to understand the prehistory of a particular literary unit. The transmission historian would of course want to find the links between the original form and the narrative as we have it, while the literary critic would attempt to answer the questions of when, how, and by whom the unit was committed to writing. The biblical theologian and the preacher can afford to bypass some of these questions, however; indeed, to some of them no answers can be found. Nevertheless, the work of the form critic has been invaluable, facilitated in this case by current knowledge of the ancient forms. While the final product results from a combination of various methods and resources, one very important element has been contributed by form-critical research. Since a great deal less is known about many other prose genres we must exercise due caution, but enough has been shown at least to validate the form-critical method.

Poetic Genres

An illustration has been provided of the way in which a form critic might approach Ps 19. We now turn to Ps 2, a psalm associated with Christ as Messiah in the NT.[33] For the Christian, the ultimate meaning of this poem is settled; either it refers in a directly prophetic sense to Jesus as Messiah, or at the very least the references to the "Son" in the psalm are legitimately applicable to the Savior. All this, however, tells nothing of the authorship, date, setting, and original context of the psalm. It is true that the apostles are reported to have attributed the psalm to David,[34] but even this fact is not directly germane to the questions asked by a form critic.

Taking the form-critical steps in order, we ask first: what structural clues enable us to define the basic literary unit? Ps 2 consists of four strophes, each with clear internal unity, and each exhibiting a certain progression of thought. The psalm begins with a rhetorical question ("Why do the nations conspire . . . ?") and ends with an ultimatum delivered to their kings. The psalm may be taken as a unit.

Second, we must determine its literary type, in this case a rather difficult question. Mowinckel[35] and others follow Gunkel in classifying it as one of a group of Royal Psalms[36] which share a common interest in the relationship between God and the king. On the one hand, this classification has certain drawbacks in that it is based largely on subject matter and draws on psalms of various standard types.[37] On the other hand, many of these Royal Psalms do not fit any of the standard types (e.g., hymn, lament, thanksgiving, blessing and curse, wisdom poem), so perhaps in this case it is still best to classify Ps 2 by its subject matter rather than its form. Its subject matter seems to suggest that it was originally composed for use at the enthronement ceremony of a new monarch. This was a time when vassal kings were likely to revolt, and the king required divine affirmation of

---

33. Acts 4:25-26; 13:33; Heb 1:5; Rev 2:27; 19:15.
34. Acts 4:25.
35. Mowinckel, *Psalms in Israel's Worship*, 1:47.
36. E.g., Pss 2, 18, 20, 21, 72, 89, 101, 110, 132, 144, as classified by Artur Weiser, *The Psalms: A Commentary*, trans. Herbert Hartwell, Old Testament Library (Philadelphia: Westminster Press, 1962), p. 63.
37. Mowinckel, *Psalms in Israel's Worship*, 1:47; A. A. Anderson, *The Book of Psalms*, New Century Bible, 2 vols. (1972; reprint ed., Grand Rapids: Wm. B. Eerdmans, 1981), 1:39.

his authority in the political world of his day. Ps 2 constitutes a series of responses by the king, the LORD, and the "chorus" to a question, "Why do the nations conspire . . . ?" It is probably best to use the term "coronation psalm"[38] so that the setting determines the type.

Step three seeks a life-setting for the genre. At this point we are limited by an inability to relate this psalm to a broad category on formal lines, but there are certainly clues within the psalm itself as to its *Sitz im Leben.* V. 6 indicates the installation of a king on Zion, the holy hill of Jerusalem, while vv. 7-8 speak of a decree by Yahweh specifically relating to the coronation of the king. The setting, then, is the coronation, whether in prospect or retrospect (v. 7 could be construed as referring to the past). Further, vv. 2 and 10 point to a time when there were vassal kings to revolt, and this situation would be truer to the occasion of Solomon's accession than to any time before or after. But the song was clearly used in more than one setting. Probably it became a kind of coronation liturgy, perhaps arising originally in the high hopes for Solomon that were generated by the Davidic covenant and later transferred to other kings who were less worthy.

Step four concerns the intent or function of the genre. In this case the original purpose is clear, namely, to celebrate the role of a king who sat as the anointed representative of Yahweh on the throne in Jerusalem. Of course, an alternate intent of the Spirit of God in the language given was to point to a coming king who would be far greater than any before Him in the line of David. But the genre itself, so far as may be determined, functioned as an affirmation of the royal son of David on the throne in Jerusalem.

Again, form criticism has brought us only part of the way. It cannot be known, for example, if this psalm ever functioned as part of a purely oral literature. But both the genre which emerges from the psalm itself and the life-setting which gave rise to the genre are evident enough to the form critic upon study of the psalm. Form-critical analysis has aided in ascertaining the function of the original genre, and the biblical theologian can from that beginning trace the glorious thread of God's promise to the ultimate Son, the one of whom it could be said, "You are the

38. Derek Kidner, *Psalms 1–72,* Tyndale Old Testament Commentaries (Downers Grove: Inter-Varsity, 1973), p. 50.

Christ, the Son of the living God" (Matt 16:16), and "This is my beloved Son; listen to him" (Mark 9:7).

Prophetic Speech

As a genre which was undoubtedly spoken before it was written, prophetic speech employs a wide range of literary forms.[39] Here, however, we are largely concerned with the common structure of the prophetic oracles themselves, and although in biblical speech patterns these prophetic oracles are usually cast in poetic form, they are sufficiently distinct from other poetry to merit study as a separate genre. Claus Westermann has divided these oracles into two categories: (1) the "prophetic judgment-speech to individuals," which is prominently featured in the historical books (e.g., 1 Kgs 11:29-40), though also found in the prophetic collections (e.g., Amos 7:14-17); and (2) the "announcement of judgment against Israel," which is seen as a stylistic development of the earlier oracle against an individual.[40] In this regard it is significant to note that the historical books were known to the Jews as "the former prophets."

While acknowledging considerable variety within the forms, Westermann discerns the basic structure of an original form from which expansions and modifications developed.[41] The basic oracle opens with an introduction which can be either the summons of a messenger (e.g., 1 Kgs 21:18-19) or the call to hear (Amos 4:1a). Second, there follows an accusation (Amos 4:1b), often with a highly developed legal indictment. Third, there comes an announcement of judgment (4:2b-3), often preceded by a messenger formula (4:2a). While there is ample room for study of each individual oracle, even a casual observer can readily see the pattern emerging. Of course, there are other forms of speech in the prophetic literature and no attempt to determine common literary patterns can or should obscure the rich variety of speech used by God's messengers of old. But the recognition of these types, and the ability to discern originally separate oracles, prayers, or accounts will help us to understand better the books as we have them now.

---

39. Koch deals with these in an extensive section (*Growth of Biblical Tradition*, pp. 183-220).
40. Claus Westermann, *Basic Forms of Prophetic Speech*, trans. H. C. White (Philadelphia: Westminster Press, 1967), chaps. 3 and 4 respectively.
41. Ibid., pp. 130-31.

Moreover, it is obvious at some points (e.g., in the dated oracles of Jeremiah) and implicit at others (e.g., Amos 7–9) that the prophetic speeches are out of chronological order. It then becomes important not only to see why they were finally arranged as they are (redaction criticism) but to ask the background and purpose of each. Thus, Amos 4:1-3 can be seen as an originally separate call to judgment on the wealthy women of Samaria, quite apart from its context in the book. As a genre, it is the simple form of messenger oracle that arose much earlier in the prophetic movement of which Amos was a part. The function or intent of the earlier oracle is also quite clear even apart from its place in Amos 4. Having established these details, we begin to ask when and why it was written down, and what principles of order may have caused it to appear in the present context.

A second example, also from Amos, will bring out another aspect of the method. Amos 5:1-17 represents in its present context the climactic center of the book. It follows hard on the stirring and sober challenge of 4:12, "prepare to meet your God, O Israel!" Chap. 5 is a funeral dirge, the form of which is plain to a reader of the Hebrew text. The extent of the unit (vv. 1-17, though probably vv. 8-9 form a separate unit) is evident from both subject matter and style. It is, however, a rather unusual dirge. The lament form is broken up by three prophetic appeals (vv. 4-5, 6-7, 14-15), each of which became part of the original form only as the inspired prophet used the old form to convey his special message of repentance and hope. The old dirge form is limited to vv. 2-3 and 16-17. Its life-setting was the simple culture of village life in Israel. A young and comely virgin is seen dying before her time; she has fallen and will not rise again. All the townsfolk and the farmers in the fields join to bewail the tragedy. The dirge is then supplemented by another form, that of the prophetic messenger oracle. The introduction (v. 1) summons the hearers. The three appeals form a call to repent and avoid the indictment. Vv. 10-12 contain the indictment itself, while the dirge becomes the announcement of judgment. Vv. 8-9 are placed at the center to unite the oracle to the remainder of the book by the recurring theme of God's power in the natural order. In v. 13 we even find a wisdom saying, quite out of place in the normal prophetic oracle but here a valid comment on the depth of Israel's hopelessness.

We have thus traced the use of old and stylized forms and their conversion into a unique and powerful literary medium in the hands of Amos. Taking the forms back to their origin illuminates their present use, and in the finished product may be better seen the richness of the medium that was employed to convey God's eternal Word to an erring nation of the eighth century.

CRITIQUE AND SUMMARY

Benefits

Considerable benefit may clearly be derived from the controlled application of a good form-critical method, for the study and classification of biblical material according to its literary type illuminates the communication process. When controlled by an objective methodology, the discovery of various life-settings has been one of the great advances in OT research, particularly with regard to the psalms. Furthermore, when kept in perspective as a preliminary study rather than as an end in itself, a form-critical analysis provides valuable material for the biblical theologian wishing to base his work on solid exegesis. It should also be remembered that form-critical analysis does not of itself determine either the historical or literary value of the material. It simply provides a tool by which the material may be better understood.

Cautions

As a general rule, two areas for caution should be noted. The first is of a literary nature: does form provide the main key to meaning, or does content? The answer must be that both make their contribution but that form-critical research can never replace the grammatical, historical, theological study of the text. Whether a particular form is used consciously or unconsciously it is merely the vehicle for that which the inspired writer wishes to convey. The medium is certainly important, but the medium is not the entire message. The second cautionary note is theologically based. It is important for the evangelical form critic not to limit his work by naturalistic presuppositions. Thus, at every stage in the process a rigid historical inquiry will be open to the working of God. Evidence for this activity may be found by normal historical inquiry, but room must be left for the supernatural acts in history of a God who revealed Himself in many and various ways to the fathers through the prophets. This note is missing in many contemporary form studies, but it should become the hallmark of evangelical interpretation.

On analyzing structure. Form-critical studies often suffer in attempting to break down the text into fragments so small that any unity of thought is lost. I would like to suggest a form criticism which can look at entire books, such as Meredith Kline's study of Deuteronomy.[42] Within a given book, the larger units may themselves be the key to form research, as shown by Herbert M. Wolf in his study of the so-called "Apology of David" in 2 Samuel.[43] Attempts to isolate every kind of formal speech unit into a separate section are not true to the fact that all speaking and writing draws for its form on a rich heritage of metaphors and idioms and at the same time depends for its content on how these are used. A final caution in analyzing structural units: the method is more easily applied to poetic or prophetic speech than to narrative material. The Genesis accounts we briefly examined are presented as part of a continuous narrative, and the formal introductions and transitions are usually those which are commonly employed by a narrator to tell his story. Using them to break up an account is not illegitimate per se, but it should be remembered that in their context they unite, not divide, the narrative.

On describing literary genres. Two cautions must be noted. First, one must avoid, so far as possible, superimposing alien modern classifications on ancient literature. This leads into the second point: current classifications often exhibit a naturalistic bias in their choice of terminology. If, for example, the terms "myth" or "saga" are defined as stories which involve primitive deities (and

---

42. Meredith G. Kline, *Treaty of the Great King* (Grand Rapids: Wm. B. Eerdmans, 1963); idem, *The Structure of Biblical Authority*, rev. ed. (Grand Rapids: Wm. B. Eerdmans, 1975).
43. Herbert M. Wolf, "The Apology of Hattušiliš Compared with Other Political Self-Justifications of the Ancient Near East" (Ph.D. diss., Brandeis University, 1967; Ann Arbor, Mich.: University Microfilms 67-16,588).

are therefore unhistorical), the application of these terms to the biblical narrative implies a contradiction of what is asserted in the text, for from a biblical point of view the direct presence of God in the action is the most important aspect of history. In such cases, the evangelical critic will either seek new categories or carefully redefine existing terms.

On discerning the life-setting. Again, caution about subjective method is required. In working with literary material as old as the Bible, the precise life-setting of a particular genre may not be recoverable. Furthermore, there may already be a perfectly clear life-setting for the unit as presented in the text, and working away from that to a hypothetical prehistoric setting may only obscure the question. For example, the account in Gen 32:24-32 provides its own *Sitz im Leben*. To work from that setting back to hypothetical reminiscences about river demons and heroic figures is of no value. Similarly, the Coronation Psalms find a reasonably coherent setting in the enthronement of Judean kings. Nothing is gained by positing festivals on pagan models for which there is no direct evidence within Israel or her literature. In the search for a life-setting, the institutions clearly pictured in Israel's own tradition must provide the basis for objective study.

On determining intent or function. Again, this must be discovered so far as possible in material from the tradition with which we are working. Because Gen 32:32 concludes with the words, "Therefore to this day the Israelites do not eat the sinew of the hip . . . ," we are justified in asking whether the genre in its original setting was not etiological (i.e., attempting to explain the origin of a phenomenon such as a name or custom). While this hardly explains the function of the narrative in its present context, it may help to illuminate a phase of the prehistory of this particular text. The clues should come from the text itself, however.

In general, then, it may be seen how valuable form-critical research can be, and evangelical interpreters can utilize these tools without violating their commitment to a high view of Scripture. That this approach has sometimes been tied to rationalistic presuppositions or subjective methodology does not in itself invalidate the discipline. Indeed, a high view of Scripture demands that all its phenomena be taken seriously, and a properly controlled form criticism provides one of the means of meeting that demand.

IV

Structural Analysis

INTRODUCTION

SINCE the mid-1960s a new star has risen on the horizon of biblical scholarship in the form of structuralism or structural analysis. As a literary rather than a historical discipline, the new structuralism has challenged traditional biblical studies at the level of its most cherished assumptions. For well over a century it has been assumed that truth from the Scriptures, if it could be gleaned at all, would derive from the intent of the writer as he addressed his own world of time and space. If the particular writing was a composite of various levels and sources, only historical research could unlock the secrets of tradition history and composition, and ultimately the theological meaning of the text. But structural analysis by its very definition seeks meaning at another level. Deliberately eschewing historical and diachronic research, structuralists claim to find in the writing itself, in the relationships of words and themes, the key to interpretation. Their focus has shifted to synchronic research in an attempt to look at the text as a given whole in all its internal and external relationships, and to assess objectively the real values inherent in the material.

Since the method originally rose quite independently of biblical studies, and because its assumptions are so alien to the latter, one might have expected the seed to find no fertile soil, but this has not been the case. In fact, many of the more notable figures engaged in research of a historical nature have welcomed structural research as an exciting new dimension to their work.

The reasons for this phenomenon are no doubt complex, but a few suggestions may be offered. The attractiveness of novelty cannot be discounted, although to argue that the trend is but one more evidence of a thirst for hearing "some new thing" is in itself too facile. Perhaps the response expresses dissatisfaction with the results of historical research, a feeling that its goal of recovering a meaningful past has not been achieved with any degree of success.[1] But there may be a further factor. A basic interest in history, so long the foundation of western intellectual endeavor, was severely challenged during the 1960s and early 1970s, and one cannot but wonder whether the new search for meaning at a nonhistorical level is related to the philosophical trends of that era.

In addition, biblical studies have recently faced a certain challenge from the secular departments of the university. Unlike the old divinity school or faculty of theology, general biblical studies exhibit a new emphasis on religious studies, and this emphasis in turn forces the discipline to justify its existence alongside the others which deal with religious phenomena. The sociologist, the anthropologist, the student of literature, and the linguist each has his own way of approaching the study of religious experience, and in a modern university there is more interchange of methods and results than there was when theologians were exclusively concerned with training men and women for service in the church. That the methodology of these other disciplines would have a profound influence on biblical studies was perhaps inevitable, and the new interest in structure may be characteristic of the coming age of religious studies. While the implications of such a trend may become more clear as the present study proceeds, only the origin of the trend is of interest at this point.

The remainder of this chapter will seek to present a brief description of structuralism as it developed in French linguistic circles early in this century, and as it evolved from that beginning through a series of modifications to the present day. A study of its assumptions and methods will be followed by a survey of how these have been applied to biblical texts, along with an attempt to distinguish those directions which have proven most fruitful.

1. E.g., Robert A. Spivey ("Structuralism and Biblical Studies: The Uninvited Guest," *Interpretation* 28 [1974]:144-45) suggests that "historical criticism of the biblical materials has not exactly covered itself with precision and clarity in the handling of the category of history — *Historie* and *Geschichte* and even *Heilsgeschichte* are slippery tales also."

Finally, I shall offer a critique of structural analysis as a tool for evangelical exegesis.

STRUCTURAL ANALYSIS: THE DISCIPLINE

Professional Semiology

Modern biblical studies in structural analysis owe their beginning to the developments in linguistic theory which followed the publication of Ferdinand de Saussure's *Cours de linguistic générale* in 1916.[2] De Saussure and those who follow him argue that language reflects certain universal patterns or structures which in turn reflect universal orders within the human brain.[3] All narrative is in some way an expression of these deep structures, and the task of the student is to discover the nature of these patterns. Since 1916, and particularly since the Second World War, various forms of theory and application have emerged in an attempt to define and develop these basic ideas.

Prominent in biblical scholarship is the name of Claude Lévi-Strauss. Although himself interested in primitive mythology and not biblical studies, Lévi-Strauss has exerted a profound influence on others who have in turn applied his method to the biblical literature.[4] In its fullest application, the work of Lévi-Strauss and other anthropologists and linguists requires a more sophisticated knowledge of linguistic theory than most biblical researchers can ever hope to command, but attempts have been made to apply portions of the method to literary sections of both Testaments. In all this activity the debt to Lévi-Strauss and other theorists such as Roland Barthes and Roman Jakobson must be acknowledged. The bibliography of technical works by these scholars is staggering, though for the biblical scholar a number of helpful analyses are available.

Perhaps the most crucial question for aspiring practitioners of the method is whether they have a sufficient grasp of what the

2. Ferdinand de Saussure, *Cours de linguistic générale* (Paris: Payot, 1916); Eng. trans. *Course in General Linguistics*, trans. Wade Baskin, ed. Charles Bally and Albert Sechehaye (New York: Philosophical Library, 1959).
3. See Richard Jacobson, "The Structuralists and the Bible," *Interpretation* 28 (1974):147.
4. See John W. Rogerson, *Myth in Old Testament Interpretation*, Beiheft zur Zeitschrift für die alttestamentliche Wissenschaft 134 (Berlin/New York: Walter de Gruyter & Co., 1974), chap. 8; Jacobson, "Structuralists and the Bible," pp. 146-47.

semiologist (structural linguist) means by structural analysis to justify inclusion of their own work under the rubric. Among professional semiologists there is still a fair measure of disagreement on the precise limits of what may be included, so a degree of flexibility must be granted. But if an accepted definition allows for excessive movement from the founding theories, the designation itself loses clear meaning.

Propositions and Assumptions

While the term "structural analysis" at times appears to signify almost any kind of textual-analytical work, the term when properly applied is a little more specific. Structural analysts, at least with reference to the system known as structuralism, would agree that the structure of language is in some way central to reality. Finding the reality reflected by structure is the true goal of analysis, and most continental structuralists have rather firm ideas about the nature of that reality. As we shall see, it is not always clear that biblical scholars using the methods of structuralism fully share this assumption, but in its purest form that is what structuralism implies.

Robert Spivey cites three assumptions that govern the subject: (1) appearance in human conduct and affairs is not reality, (2) reality is structured, and (3) the structuring is codelike.[5] Regarding the text or its contents as the appearance, the structuralist will attempt to look behind or below the text to discover the deeper structure which may reflect reality. Lévi-Strauss uses the analogy of geology, in which the substratum that is basic and fundamental runs beneath the surface of the landscape. Likewise, beyond the world of discourse and rationality, there is "a category at once more important and more valid, that is, the meaningful."[6] Put into the language of de Saussure, the text or individual utterance (*parole*) is governed by a code (*langue*), and it is this code which the endeavor seeks, for it is at this level that reality may be approached or apprehended.[7]

While there is little agreement on the precise nature of the structure or shape of reality, all structuralists would agree *inter*

5. Spivey, "Structuralism and Biblical Studies," p. 134, following Donald G. MacRae, Introduction to Raymond Boudon, *The Uses of Structuralism*, trans. Michelina Vaughan (London: Heinemann, 1971), p. ix.
6. Spivey, "Structuralism and Biblical Studies," p. 138.
7. See Jacobson, "Structuralists and the Bible," p. 147.

alia that such a structure exists. For Claude Lévi-Strauss, following the Prague linguist Roman Jakobson, the basic aspect of human thought is to be found in the concept of binary opposition. All language, learning, and development are thus subjected to a pervasive Hegelian dialectical analysis. It is true that Noam Chomsky, among others, has rejected this as an oversimplification,[8] and Lévi-Strauss himself has apparently entertained doubts about the comprehensive nature of the paradigm. Using the model of the traffic light, he now finds that although red and green are binary opposites, the yellow light mediates between the two. In the same way, human expression, though essentially formed on the binary model, incorporates various mediating or integrating elements at many levels.[9] Even this model may be oversimplified, and Lévi-Strauss later speaks rather of an *esprit* which, according to Edmund Leach, "appears as part of an extremely involved interchange relationship."[10]

Roland Barthes is even less definite about the nature of the structure. The semiologist determines "what relations the text establishes, what its rules of organization may be, how it *allows* for meaning,"[11] but from that beginning he goes on to reflect on the rules of discourse (*langue*) in the context of the text, and this analysis should lead to "formalized, exhaustive, and simple statements of the nonconscious determination of the text."[12] If this sounds more nebulous than the argument of Lévi-Strauss, it at least has the advantage of flexibility. Barthes has demonstrated what he means, finding a great range of ambiguity and paradox in the story of Jacob at the Jabbok in Gen 32:23-32,[13] and it is presumably at this level that we are to look for those universal

8. John Lyons, *Chomsky* (London: Fontana, 1970), pp. 84-85; cited in Spivey, "Structuralism and Biblical Studies," p. 141.
9. See Spivey, "Structuralism and Biblical Studies," p. 140; cf. Rogerson, *Myth in OT Interpretation*, p. 105; Jacobson, "Structuralists and the Bible," p. 156.
10. Edmund Leach, "The Legitimacy of Solomon," in *Genesis as Myth and Other Essays* (London: Jonathan Cape, 1969), p. 25; quoted in Jacobson, "Structuralists and the Bible," p. 156.
11. Paraphrased by Jacobson, "Structuralists and the Bible," p. 158; from Roland Barthes, "La lutte avec l'ange," in *Analyse structurale et exégèse biblique*, ed. F. Bovon (Neuchâtel: Delachaux et Niestlé, 1971), p. 28; Eng. trans. "The Struggle with the Angel," *Structural Analysis and Biblical Exegesis*, trans. Alfred M. Johnson, Jr., Pittsburgh Theological Monograph Series 3 (Pittsburgh: Pickwick Press, 1974), p. 22.
12. Jacobson, "Structuralists and the Bible," p. 158, with reference to Barthes.
13. In "The Struggle with the Angel"; see Jacobson, "Structuralists and the Bible," p. 158.

structures by which reality is determined. Barthes does not pretend that he can find a single "scientific" paradigm, but speaks rather of "plural, overlapping codes."[14] Of course, the problem for newcomers to the discipline is that these "codes" tend to be obvious only to the fertile mind of Roland Barthes, and we are left still wondering just what the nature of this structure may be. The structualist often begins with a rather definite world view, which in turn colors his assumptions upon approaching the text. Lévi-Strauss is not alone in basing his dialectical structures on a Marxist and Freudian analysis,[15] for Barthes also looks to both Marx and Freud for his basic paradigms.[16] But surely there are non-Marxist and non-Freudian ways of analyzing the primitive consciousness of an author, whether the material is myth (as in the work of Lévi-Strauss) or modern narrative (so Barthes). Thus, even before looking at method, one must ask what philosophical presuppositions influence the approach of the analyst.

METHOD

Synchronic and Diachronic Research

Basic to the method, though still a subject of debate, is a concern for synchronic rather than diachronic research. Whereas traditional exegesis has attempted to answer questions about the historical process by which a text was produced, including either the intention of its author or community, or the social context out of which it arose, synchronic exegesis looks for another dimension. The text is seen as a literary product, a given entity which does not merely reflect its own time and circumstances, but at a deeper level conveys a symbolic and timeless structure or meaning. Thus the object of the research is to discover how the text produces meaning, rather than how the text may have been produced.[17]

Whereas traditional exegesis has looked at the process author-to-text, synchronic exegesis looks at the process text-to-reader. This is a slight oversimplification, however, for most semiologists

14. Hugh C. White, "French Structuralism and OT Narrative Analysis: Roland Barthes," *Semeia* 3 (1975):101.
15. See Spivey, "Structuralism and Biblical Studies," p. 137.
16. See White, "Structuralism and OT," pp. 100 and 120.
17. Ibid., p. 101.

would even reject the concept of a "history of interpretation" approach on the grounds that it is as rigidly historical as traditional diachronic exegesis. The universal, timeless structures are to be pursued, not the ways in which meaning has previously been discovered. A structuralist with a strongly antihistorical bias, like Lévi-Strauss,[18] shows the tendency most clearly in his preference for "myth" over the study of historical narrative, for it is in myth that the historical dimension most readily gives way to the universal and the timeless.

Whether such an approach can ever be reconciled or viewed as complementary to historical research remains an open question. The majority of biblical scholars who espouse literary-structural methods remain convinced that synchronic and diachronic research are two sides of one coin,[19] although caution has been expressed as to whether the new approach may not by definition or default exclude historical concerns.[20]

On the positive side, there is undoubtedly much to be gained by taking a fresh look at the text itself, at its internal and external relationships, and at its effect on hearer or reader. A brief survey of work on OT passages will show the gains in understanding that have been derived, and it would appear that nothing done by a biblical scholar (in contrast, e.g., to Edmund Leach) exhibits the kind of antihistorical bias which is an integral part of the anthropological system of Lévi-Strauss. The question is not whether this kind of synchronic research might be useful; compared to much of the arid irrelevance and speculation of recent form-critical endeavor it shines all the more brightly. More to the point is whether the recent work, when separated from the antihistorical world view of the semiologist, can properly be called structuralism.

To summarize the first point on method: structural analysis bypasses the history of the text to concentrate on its structure. The special problem of what might actually constitute a given text will be examined later in this study.

18. Spivey, "Structuralism and Biblical Studies," pp. 143-45.

19. E.g., Daniel Patte, *What Is Structural Exegesis?*, Guides to Biblical Scholarship, New Testament Series (Philadelphia: Fortress Press, 1976), pp. 84-85; Dan O. Via, Jr., in the Editor's Foreword to *What Is Structural Exegesis?*, p. iv.

20. Spivey, "Structuralism and Biblical Studies," pp. 143-45; James Barr, *The Bible in the Modern World* (London: SCM Press, 1973), pp. 63-65.

Steps in Structural Exegesis

The first question that must be answered by the prospective practitioner, then, is whether he intends his structural analysis truly to grow out of the philosophical system which we have described as structural*ism*. At this point biblical scholars fall into various categories. Daniel Patte, for example, represents those few who have made an attempt to understand and reproduce the system of French linguistic science. Although conceding that "this work has just begun,"[21] Patte goes on to apply the system of A. J. Greimas on narrative structures to the parable of the Good Samaritan, while he employs the model of Lévi-Strauss on mythical structures to analyze Gal 1:1-10![22] By contrast, R. C. Culley attempts to apply some insights from the method, but confesses that he is not ready to radically reevaluate "the question of history and the problem of the subject." He opts instead for a less stringent analytical method which "does not assume the broader framework of structuralism."[23] Culley would seem to represent the majority of OT scholars, but we must look at both approaches before appraising the integrity of each method.

A. J. Greimas's narrative structure. For Greimas, narrative is that which evokes the value "narrativity,"[24] and in his structure, six "hierarchically distinct elements" are distinguished. These are sequence, syntagm, statement, actantial model, function, and actant.[25] The terms and their definitions are highly technical, presupposing a fairly sophisticated knowledge of linguistic theory.

First, the narrative is viewed as a series of *sequences*:

—initial sequence (related to the final)
  —optional disrupting subsequence
  —one or several topical sequences
—a final sequence (related to the initial)[26]

---

21. Patte, *What Is Structural Exegesis?*, p. 35.
22. Ibid., chaps. 3 and 4 respectively.
23. Robert C. Culley, "Structural Analysis: Is it Done with Mirrors?", *Interpretation* 28 (1974):169.
24. See Patte, *What Is Structural Exegesis?*, p. 36.
25. Ibid., p. 37. (For a list of Greimas's major publications, see ibid., pp. 36-37 n. 2, and the Annotated Bibliography, p. 86.
26. Adapted from Patte, *What Is Structural Exegesis?*, p. 37.

The subsequence, when present, explains how the initial sequence is opposed or disrupted; in this case, one or more of the topical sequences is concerned to show how the opposition is overcome in order to *fulfill* the initial sequence. In the parable which Patte employs to illustrate the method (Luke 10:30-35), the action of the man going down to Jericho forms the initial sequence, and that of the robbers a disrupting subsequence. The initial sequence sets the agenda for the rest of the narrative. Here topical sequences about priest, Levite, and Samaritan follow to fulfill the initial sequence; the first two fail, and the third succeeds.[27]

Second, each sequence breaks down into a succession of three narrative *syntagms*, namely, a *contract* syntagm, a *disjunction/conjunction* syntagm, and a *performance* syntagm. In simplified form, the syntagms represent individualized actions of a stylized nature, and these make up the sequence. For example, the act of compassion is the contract syntagm, the approach to the wounded man is the element of disjunction/conjunction, and the remainder of the Samaritan's actions collectively represent the performance syntagm.

Third, every syntagm is broken down into narrative *statements*, each of which may be compared to a basic sentence with a bare subject and predicate: someone (or something) performs an act to carry out the syntagm. In the performance syntagm of Patte's example, the narrative statements would include "bound up his wounds," "pouring on oil and wine," etc.[28]

Fourth, each such action is assigned to a technical category of description called a *canonical function*, such as arrival, departure, conjunction, disjunction, acceptance, refusal, confrontation, etc. Those in the Good Samaritan parable include acceptance ("he had compassion") and conjunction ("and went to him").[29]

Fifth, the roles of those who perform (or are acted on by) the various functions are classified in one of six *actantial roles*, or, more commonly, *actants*. These are Sender, Receiver, Subject, Object, Helper, and Opponent, and all of these are implicit or explicit in each narrative. (The person who manifests, or performs, a

27. Ibid., p. 38.
28. Ibid., pp. 39-40.
29. Ibid., pp. 40-41. Patte here cites the discussion by Jean Calloud, *Structural Analysis of Narrative*, trans. D. Patte, Semeia Supplements 4 (Philadelphia: Fortress Press; Missoula, Mo.: Scholars Press, 1976).

given actant may be called the *actor*.) At various points in Patte's example, the Samaritan is found in the role of the Subject, the wounded man that of the Receiver, his welfare that of the Object, the robbers that of the Opponent, and the oil, wine, donkey, etc. that of the Helper. The Sender is in this case unknown, unless it is viewed as providence or some other force.[30]

Sixth, the relationships among the various functions and actants are described by building an *actantial model*, and at this point the first level of the structural analysis has been completed.[31]

It will be seen that use of such a model, even at the level of simple analysis, requires a measure of training in the method. But what is required at this level is little compared to what is required at the next level. As Patte has observed, "By itself the analysis of a single text in terms of the narrative structure yields very limited results."[32] The exegesis is now carried into the realm of mythical structures and ultimately to a semantic analysis, and for these Patte turns to the model provided by Lévi-Strauss.

C. Lévi-Strauss's mythical structure. Basic to this step is the belief that certain universal structures operate in all human discourse. For Lévi-Strauss, myth differs from narrative or other nonmythical material only in that its deep structures come more readily to the surface.[33] But the view of reality that allows for an analysis of myth is all-pervasive; thus Patte can apply it to both a theological argument (Gal 1:1-10) and the parable of the Good Samaritan.

Mythical exegesis aims to uncover the "deep structures" operating in the consciousness of the myth. Lévi-Strauss himself prefers to group together all the mythological texts of a given culture, feeling that all are variations of a basic myth which he defines as the sum of all its variants.[34] To find the basic mythical structure, Lévi-Strauss attempts to reduce the events of the story to short sentences called *mythemes*, each of which may be symbolized by the formula $F_x(a)$ and read, "a function 'x' is linked

30. Patte, *What Is Structural Exegesis?*, pp. 41-42.
31. Ibid.
32. Ibid., p. 52.
33. Ibid., p. 59.
34. Claude Lévi-Strauss, "The Structural Study of Myth," in *Structural Anthropology*, trans. Clare Jacobson and Brooke Grundfest Schoepf (Garden City, N.Y.: Basic Books, 1963), p. 213; cited by Patte, *What Is Structural Exegesis?*, p. 55.

to a given subject (or state) 'a'."[35] Groups of these mythemes may often be found in a given text, and from the grouping of related mythemes Lévi-Strauss isolates broader mythemes, that is, new mythemes which express in broader terms what several constituent mythemes had implicitly expressed.

Here the progression seems to work in reverse of A. J. Greimas's narrative exegesis, where the largest units of structure (the sequences) are broken down into smaller parts in a hierarchical structure. Lévi-Strauss goes from the smaller to the more comprehensive, working all the time toward that comprehensive view of reality by which he analyzes all human endeavor. The concept of fundamental polarity with mediating factors constantly at work (as in the traffic light model) seems always to be the basic result of the analysis. Even in nonmythological texts, although the process is more lengthy, the result is the same.

Patte applies the methods of Lévi-Strauss first to Paul's theological argument in Gal 1:1-10, though he admits at the beginning that the form of this text is very different from that of myth. The latter is characterized by an unconscious expression of the myth, and marked by redundancies (i.e., separate versions of the same story) rather than a logical chain of development.

Nevertheless, in the theological argument the basic unit is still the mytheme. Unlike the mythical text, however, in which story functions are reduced to short sentences, in the theological text each short Pauline phrase must be expanded to find its value as a mytheme. Thus the phrase "Paul an apostle" is really composed of two mythemes standing in opposition: "Paul as the common man" and "Paul as an apostle" make up one broad mytheme which incorporates the two into a fundamental opposition.[36] The key to the structure is found not simply in the mythemes but in the way they are mediated in a relationship of fundamental opposition. Patte includes a diagram which shows how "proclamation by Paul" moderates between "Galatians as slaves to an evil aeon" and "Galatians as Christians." The resurrection mediates between the Lord Jesus Christ and the dead Jesus, and so forth. From these mediated oppositions the basic mythical structure emerges, and in this case the "gospel as teaching" and the

35. Patte, *What Is Structural Exegesis?*, p. 55, following Lévi-Strauss, *Structural Anthropology*, p. 207.

36. Patte, *What Is Structural Exegesis?*, pp. 60 and 64.

"other gospel" opposition is seen as fundamental to the whole.[37] The person of Paul, his experience, and his argument are seen as mediating the various oppositions. But the basic code is in the oppositions, and Patte suggests that the method will lead to a number of as yet unexplored "hermeneutical possibilities."[38]

Perhaps by this point it will be apparent that the method of the true French structuralist remains the province of only a select number of initiates. The method seems to be touched by an esoteric gnosticism which requires the scholar to give a priori consent to a view of reality which he might otherwise not have shared. Whether there is a universal "myth" and whether it can be reduced to simple formulas will remain open questions to most students of the biblical literature. Perhaps, however, this review of Patte's little book illustrates the method such that one may understand why most biblical scholars have looked for modifications or alternatives.

Other "Structural" Methods

Other methods currently employed in the pursuit of what is called "structural exegesis," particularly in OT circles, merit our attention. It will be seen that the terminology of French structuralism is utilized or ignored in varying degrees, and that this group is unified largely by the fact that its members are willing to look at the text synchronically. Robert Culley probably speaks for all when he says his analysis "does not assume the broader framework of structuralism. Whether this means that my work may not qualify as 'structural analysis' remains to be seen."[39] When freed from the rigid methodological assumptions of Greimas and Lévi-Strauss (as illustrated in the field of biblical studies by the work of Patte, Edmund Leach, and others), structural exegesis has taken a variety of directions. What follows will be an attempt to classify these directions, and to describe briefly the methods employed.

R. C. Culley. Robert Culley has published a series of articles

37. Ibid., p. 70 and fig. 4.
38. Ibid., p. 75.
39. Robert C. Culley, "Structural Analysis: Is it Done with Mirrors?", *Interpretation* 28 (1974):169 (italics added).

in which he tentatively pursues a method for the structural analysis of a text. In a paper delivered to the 1971 Uppsala Congress,[40] Culley initially offers a critique of Edmund Leach. Recognizing that Leach follows Lévi-Strauss in denying that surface structure contains the key to analysis, Culley rightly asks if anyone not committed to a view of the all-pervasive role of binary opposites would also discover the deep structures discovered by Leach in the Garden of Eden narrative. While he raises further questions about meaning, Culley gives no hint of how he might do structural research himself.

Three years later, Culley published an article in which he distinguishes his own development of structural analysis from that of structuralism as a world view on the one hand, and from rhetorical criticism as an investigation concerned only with stylistic features on the other. Structural analysis, by contrast, "directs attention rather to exploring other kinds of patterns in the text relating to things like narrative action, the relationships of characters, as well as many other aspects of texts such as temporal and spatial frameworks." A hint of Culley's own tentative view of all this may be found in the next statement: "it appears that structural analysis may be viewed as something more than just another way to analyze texts."[41]

Without agreeing to the presuppositions of structuralism, Culley clearly feels the method should go beyond mere stylistic or rhetorical criticism. He gives a short example to illustrate what structural analysis on these terms might look like, and a fuller expression of his ideas appears in two later studies. A short article analyzes three groups of brief biblical stories (miracle, deception, and punishment stories),[42] while *Studies in the Structure of Hebrew Narrative*[43] combines questions on a common framework or structure in miracle stories with a concern for the oral development of those accounts.

The former may be used to illustrate his method. First, Culley

40. Culley, "Some Comments on Structural Analysis and Biblical Studies," published in *Congress Volume: Uppsala*, Vetus Testamentum Supplements 22 (Leiden: E. J. Brill, 1972), pp. 129-42.
41. Culley, "Structural Analysis," p. 169.
42. Culley, "Themes and Variations in Three Groups of OT Narratives," *Semeia* 3 (1975):3-13.
43. Culley, *Studies in the Structure of Hebrew Narrative*, Semeia Supplements 3 (Philadelphia: Fortress Press; Missoula, Mo.: Scholars Press, 1976).

follows Lévi-Strauss in juxtaposing all possible examples of a type within a given body of literature: since some types overlap (i.e., common elements may be found in miracle, deception, and punishment stories), the groups will not always appear homogeneous. But Culley makes it clear that "these labels are not meant to indicate genre";[44] his concern is not with origins but with structures. Having grouped his stories, Culley proceeds (1) "to see what relationships can be detected among the stories within each of the groups," and (2) "to see what relationships can be seen among the groups themselves."[45] In the miracle stories he finds a common pattern, "problem-miracle/solution," while in the seven deception stories the pattern is "problem-deception/solution." (Incidentally, a fundamental literary trait may perhaps be observed in Culley's article, which concludes with seven punishment stories — three sets of perfect sevens.)

To this point there are no surprises, but Culley's alignment with structuralism proper is more explicit in the next step. In attempting to move from the surface to the deep structures (though Culley does not use this terminology), he finds a fundamental opposition between life and death in each group of stories, with the movements going in both directions. Again with echoes from French structuralism, Culley proposes a mediation of some kind in each story. Meaning is presumably achieved at this stage, although nothing is made of the life/death syndrome as a universal human structure. (That point, however, could be readily granted, since death, along with taxes, is a universal given.)

More questionable is Culley's finding death as a major motif in each of the stories. Among the miracle accounts, three of the seven deal with making bitter or poison liquid drinkable, two more deal with a dead boy restored to life and with a dead man's widow, and the sixth presents a miracle in which water prevents death from overtaking the people of Israel in the desert.[46] But the seventh, the floating axe head narrative of 2 Kgs 6:1-7, has only (in Culley's words) "a vague association with death because it shares a pattern with the other stories."[47] But the pattern itself

44. Culley, "Three Groups of OT Narratives," p. 4.
45. Ibid., p. 3.
46. Moses at Marah, Exod 15:22-26; Elisha and the spring, 2 Kgs 2:19-22; Elisha and the pottage, 2 Kgs 4:38-41; Elijah and the dead boy, 1 Kgs 17:17-24; Elisha and the widow, 2 Kgs 4:1-7; Moses at Massah and Meribah, Exod 17:1-7.
47. Culley, "Three Groups of OT Narratives," p. 7.

is not what has led to the "death/life" deep structure; the pattern only talks about miracles as a solution to a few stereotyped problems. In Groups II and III of Culley's analysis the "death" structure is even more forced: Lot's two daughters (Gen 19:30-38) and Tamar (Gen 38) are faced with childlessness, which "can be understood as a form of death."[48] At this point Culley stops, but we are left with the feeling that his own analysis on the level of ultimate meaning has become as subjective as that of Edmund Leach, of whose work he once wrote a perceptive critique. Leach at least began with a world view that determined his result. Culley, while rejecting the framework of Lévi-Strauss and Leach, is no more convincing when his own analysis brings their dialectical conclusions to the surface of the text.

R. Polzin. A second Canadian scholar has espoused structural analysis in a series of publications. Robert Polzin of Carleton University, unlike many of the newer structural analysts, is not slow to criticize both form and source analysis as "counterproductive."[49] Polzin employs structural categories more than some of his colleagues, though he points out that a full science of discourse has not yet been formulated. As a contributor to the *Interpretation* symposium on method, Polzin has provided a reasonably complete statement of his principles,[50] and a recent publication further shows how he would approach a series of pentateuchal narratives.[51]

In his work on Job, Polzin speaks of "three elements which we would consider fundamental to a structural analysis," namely, the "framework," the "code," and the "message" of the book, and he relates these categories to the structural distinctions of A. J. Greimas and Roman Jakobson.[52]

The first step, that of establishing the framework, involves dividing the discourse into its largest (rather than smallest) units, which division Polzin undertakes like Barthes at the "functional

48. Ibid., p. 8.
49. Robert Polzin, "The Framework of the Book of Job," *Interpretation* 28 (1974):183, particularly as applied to Job. See also his criticism of Klaus Koch's *Formgeschichtliche* analyses of Gen 12, 20, and 26 in " 'The Ancestress of Israel' in Danger," *Semeia* 3 (1975):81-83.
50. Cf. his discussion in "Framework of Job," pp. 186-89.
51. Polzin, "Ancestress of Israel" (pp. 81-98).
52. Polzin, "Framework of Job," p. 187 and n. 9.

level."[53] In the framework of Job, Polzin finds four "movements" which correspond to four functions in the story, and these "mediate some conflict or contradiction."[54] Although these movements happen to correspond to an outline of the book of Job,[55] the sequential order is not necessary to the analysis. Within the movements, various "lower" sequences are discovered, working down to what are called the "cardinal functions" on which the entire structure rests.[56] This part of Polzin's analysis is not unlike the conventional exercise of outlining the book, although his functional approach definitely reflects his observation of "mediated conflicts" at the heart of the discursive movements.

A second step, mentioned but not illustrated, is the use of the "paradigmatic pattern" isolated in the study of the framework to discover the *code*.[57] At this stage, we pass from the surface structures to the "deep structures" which reflect reality. Note that a certain element of opposition has already been discovered in Job (though Polzin does not use that term), and I am sure this will be basic to the true code which will emerge. Here, presumably, one enters the world of *langue*,[58] where the universals of human behavior emerge from beneath the surface of human discourse.

The third step, that of determining the *message*, "would treat those aspects of the book (besides its components and its system) which must be known before its message(s) can be grasped."[59] While the code involves universal invariables, the message is external to the text and relates to the world at large, rather than to the world of the myth or discourse in question.

The example cited above demonstrates Polzin's method in analyzing a long, unified poem like Job, and another slant is added in a study of Gen 12, 20, and 26.[60] Here he rejects both form and source analysis, and the method by which he then proceeds appears to have three steps.

53. Ibid., p. 187 and n. 10.
54. Ibid., p. 190.
55. Job's affliction (1–37); the vision of God (38:1–42:6); the conflict resolved by God's word (42:7-8); Job's restoration (42:10-15).
56. Polzin, "Framework of Job," p. 189.
57. Ibid., p. 200.
58. Ibid., p. 187 n. 9.
59. Ibid., p. 188.
60. Polzin, "Ancestress of Israel."

First, Polzin looks for "transformations" within the three versions of the same basic story. A transformation, as far as I can determine, is a point at which the ongoing context of the "story line," as unfolded in the book of Genesis, leads to a change of detail or movement from one story to the next. Thus in Gen 12 Abraham begins with neither wealth nor progeny. In chap. 20 he has acquired wealth but still lacks progeny, and the context of chaps. 12–20 makes it clear that he is destined to have both. This different starting point or transformation is basic to the literary development or plot of the book. In Gen 26 Isaac is now the ancestor of Israel, and he has progeny but not wealth, so the theme is kept alive but transformed with a fresh dimension. Over against the starting point of each incident, the role of the irregular relationship is also seen to undergo a transformation, although in each case it functions as an obstacle to the actualization of God's blessing on the patriarch. These transformations are all diagrammed structurally, and they appear to represent the level of surface structure or "framework" that was described in Polzin's earlier treatment of Job.[61]

A second step is the formulation of structural laws, presumably now at the level of deep structure.[62] These, however, still seem to be able to operate at the level of the story itself, for the structural laws are those "according to which wealth, progeny, and blessing by God are able to be connected in the patriarchal narratives."[63]

After other transformations have been isolated, a third step relates the various transformations to one another. Transformations about receiving blessing, for example, are related to transformations concerning the way in which mankind discerns the will of Yahweh.[64] Polzin's article, which provides a fine example of thematic or stylistic analysis, follows his earlier work but stops at what the linguists would call the surface level. The variants and invariables are concisely catalogued and set over against one another, but little in the analysis goes beyond the surface structure to the deeper realities hinted at in his earlier work.

---

61. Ibid., pp. 81, 83-88.
62. Ibid., p. 88.
63. Ibid., p. 89.
64. Ibid., pp. 95-96.

Summary. Culley and Polzin have been cited at some length because they seem representative of OT scholars who adopt certain structural methods. Culley is typical of a group which would (1) openly reject the label and philosophical framework of structuralism but still use something of its synchronic methods; and (2) attempt to relate structural exegesis in some fashion to diachronic research, especially form criticism. Polzin, although beginning with a philosophical disavowal of structuralism, more openly espouses the theory in his methodological construct. In some ways, his attempt to be a true structuralist is more thorough, for he clearly bypasses any significant amount of historical research. But even Polzin does not go all the way: his finished product is closer to what has increasingly come to be designated "rhetorical criticism" or "style criticism" than to the true structural analysis of the French scholars as reflected in Patte and some NT exegetes.

Other examples of the same general category might be cited but the results would show only varying proportions of the same combinations. Of particular interest to pentateuchal research, however, are monographs by J. P. Fokkelman, George W. Coats, and Sean McEvenue.[65] Although these writers differ in method and conclusions, they would all align themselves more closely to Culley and Polzin, rather than follow the structuralists as closely as Patte has, or in another form as Edmund Leach has tried to do.

Literary Approaches and Structural Analysis

Before moving to other questions raised by structural analysts, we should briefly look at other contemporary "literary" approaches, especially those that might be confused with structural exegesis. Martin Kessler, for example, a student of James Muilenburg, argues that "structural analysis" has become an unfortunate rubric for synchronic literary methodology, for it "may easily be confused with structuralism, associated with Pi-

---

65. J. P. Fokkelman, *Narrative Art in Genesis: Specimens of Stylistic and Structural Analysis*, trans. Puck Visser-Hagedoorn (Assen and Amsterdam: Van Gorcum, 1975); George W. Coats, *From Canaan to Egypt: Structural and Theological Context for the Joseph Story*, Catholic Biblical Quarterly Monograph Series 3 (Washington: Catholic Biblical Association of America, 1976); Sean E. McEvenue, *The Narrative Style of the Priestly Writer*, Analecta Biblica 50 (Rome: Biblical Institute Press, 1971). See below for further discussion of Fokkelman and Coats.

aget and Lévi-Strauss, and the literary critic, Roland Barthes."[66]

Rhetorical criticism. To describe the kind of literary approach which operates without structuralist philosophical presuppositions, Muilenburg has proposed the term "rhetorical criticism." Without rejecting either form research or an interest in the original author or setting, Muilenburg goes on to affirm,

> What I am interested in, above all, is in understanding the nature of Hebrew literary composition, in exhibiting the structural patterns that are employed for the fashioning of a literary unit, whether in poetry or in prose, and in discerning the many and various devices by which the predications are formulated and ordered into a unified whole. Such an enterprise I should describe as rhetoric and the methodology as rhetorical criticism.[67]

This enterprise is some distance removed from that of the followers of Lévi-Strauss, and much closer to that of scholars like Culley and Polzin. Muilenburg's method requires the user (1) to define the limit or scope of the literary unit using its literary features;[68] and (2) "to recognize the structure of a composition and to discern the configuration of its component parts, to delineate the warp and woof out of which the literary fabric is woven, and to note the various rhetorical devices that are employed."[69] A stress on literary features replaces the binary oppositions of Lévi-Strauss, while the absence of a theory of deep structures and codes further puts this approach in a category different from that of the French structuralist. These differences, however, should not prevent one from observing the similarities that remain, especially as they relate to the methods employed by biblical scholars.

Others. While others have not responded to the designation "rhetorical criticism," Muilenburg and his students have not been alone in calling for a literary approach to biblical exegesis. Edwin M. Good has argued for a strict separation between source and literary analysis, reserving the latter term for Muilenburg's

66. Martin Kessler, *Semitics* 4 (1974):32.
67. James Muilenburg, "Form Criticism and Beyond," *Journal of Biblical Literature* 88 (1969):8.
68. Ibid., pp. 8-10.
69. Ibid., p. 10.

rhetorical criticism.[70] At the same time, James Barr has taken up the question by critiquing several continental and British movements and suggesting that questions of theology and meaning must be combined with any literary approach;[71] he cites the works of Luis Alonso-Schökel as a model for such discussion. Yet another designation — "Total Interpretation" — has been suggested by the Israeli scholar Meir Weiss, who looks at structural analysis as a literary approach to Hebrew poetry.[72] Finally, a recent Fortress Guide by David Robertson is appropriately titled *The Old Testament and the Literary Critic*. Robertson here appears to have eliminated historical and theological categories altogether (though admitting that these are often "alternative methodologies"), in favor of viewing the Bible as "imaginative literature."[73] The success of his imaginative approach can be seen in his analysis of Exod 1– 15 as a slightly defective type of early comedy in which, it is true, the hero wins, but in which the implicit world view is morally oversimplified to the extent that it is not acceptable to mature adults.[74]

Structural Analysis in the Pentateuch

Roland Barthes on Gen 32:22-32. This brief survey of recent structuralist work on the Pentateuch will begin by looking at the contribution of structuralists rather than biblical scholars. The short essay "La lutte avec l'ange" by the literary critic Roland Barthes, now available in English,[75] provides a good place to begin, and it might be read in conjunction with a helpful critique by Hugh C. White.[76]

Although he does not openly espouse any kind of source or form analysis, Barthes approaches the story of Jacob and his

70. See his review of Norman Habel, *Literary Criticism of the Old Testament* in *Journal of Biblical Literature* 92 (1973):288-89.

71. James Barr, "Reading the Bible as Literature," *Bulletin of the John Rylands Library* 56 (1973):10-33. (For a short list of Alonso-Schökel's relevant publications, see ibid., p. 31 n. 1.)

72. Meir Weiss, "Die Methode der 'Total Interpretation'," *Congress Volume: Uppsala*, Vetus Testamentum Supplements 22 (Leiden: E. J. Brill, 1972), pp. 88-112. Cf. Barr, "Bible as Literature," pp. 24-25.

73. David Robertson, *The Old Testament and the Literary Critic*, Guides to Biblical Scholarship, Old Testament Series (Philadelphia: Fortress Press, 1977), p. 4.

74. Ibid., pp. 28-32.

75. See n. 11 above.

76. See n. 14 above.

opponent as a type of folklore or myth in which the patriarch is opposed at the river by some form of genie. In fact, he discovers "two different possibilities of reading"[77] which could, as White points out,[78] parallel Gunkel's "sources." Barthes, however, views these discrepancies not as options from which the "original" must be selected but rather as two equally valid ways of reading. (1) If Jacob has not yet crossed the river, his struggle is to overcome the dragon (obstacle) and cross victoriously. This is the folklorist option, and it contains a certain degree of structural decisiveness and finality. (2) If Jacob had already crossed the obstacle, the struggle is not decisive in the structure, but "only a pause between a position of immobility . . . and a marching movement,"[79] or, as White paraphrases, "only a momentary detention in the midst of a passage from one place to another."[80] As a result, two different but complete structures are distinguished here; each is made up of a series of three sequences (the crossing, the struggle, the change of name), and both are set together in a context of paradox and ambiguity.[81] As the heart of his analysis Barthes explores the meaning attached to this ambiguity, in contrast to the form critics who were forced to opt for one of the two putative tales.

Up to the point of his discovery and analysis of structural features Barthes disavows any discovery of meaning, but building on the symbolic aspect of the ambiguity of structure he turns briefly to the structural theories of Greimas and Propp for a deeper level of significance.[82] It is only at this level that Barthes would call his work *structural* analysis; for the earlier phase he uses the term *sequential* analysis or even *textual* analysis.

This latter point should be emphasized, for in his sequential analysis (of surface structures) Barthes's method and conclusions are not alien to the world of biblical studies; although students of the OT might arrive at varying conclusions, they would do so by essentially similar methods. In the application of the structural theories of Lévi-Strauss, Propp, and Greimas, however, the

77. Barthes, "Struggle with the Angel," p. 24.
78. White, "Structuralism and OT," p. 105.
79. Barthes, "Struggle with the Angel," p. 26.
80. White, "Structuralism and OT," p. 108.
81. Ibid., pp. 26-27; cf. Jacobson, "Structuralists and the Bible," pp. 158-59.
82. Barthes, "Struggle with the Angel," pp. 30-33.

object is no longer to understand a particular narrative or combination of narratives in a historical setting or settings. Rather, the task is to relate the narrative to a universal set of values expressed in the "mythical" world view of the linguist. The struggle with the angel has passed now from the world of biblical revelation to the world of universal mythology, and the latter, not the former, is viewed as the realm of meaning.

Edmund Leach on Gen 1–4. Perhaps the most celebrated foray into the world of pentateuchal studies by a structuralist came in 1961, when the Cambridge social anthropologist Edmund Leach wrote his first essay applying the methods of Lévi-Strauss to the Genesis account of the Garden of Eden.[83] Although Leach's work has been amply critiqued by John Rogerson and Robert Culley,[84] among others, it must nevertheless be mentioned as a pure if somewhat eccentric representative of structuralist method. It should be noted that Lévi-Strauss himself would not have applied his method to a text like Genesis,[85] for he believed that a single written form of a historically conditioned text was too far removed from basic structures to reflect the true meanings. Leach is fully aware of this, but argues that the restraint is unnecessarily cautious.

Leach begins by setting aside almost all the research on Genesis done by others. No attention is given to source analysis, nor even to philological research and linguistic study (the *KJV* is used throughout), and even the surface or sequential analysis of the text is bypassed as being without great importance.[86] Thus, the areas of structural analysis which have occupied most biblical studies (the surface structure) give way for an *immediate* search for the deep structures of Lévi-Strauss, namely, the pairs of binary oppositions mediated by other elements in the myth. By this rearrangement along paradigmatic lines an entire series of such pairs emerges, and the basic structure of Lévi-Strauss's world view is vindicated. Culley has quite rightly contrasted this new structure and emphasis with that of the Genesis texts them-

83. Edmund Leach, "Genesis as Myth," in *Genesis as Myth and Other Essays* (London: Jonathan Cape, 1969).
84. Rogerson, *Myth in OT Interpretation*, pp. 109-12; Culley, "Comments on Structural Analysis," p. 137.
85. Rogerson, *Myth in OT Interpretation*, p. 109.
86. Culley, "Comments on Structural Analysis," p. 137.

selves,[87] so the present critique does not need to go further. Whether this kind of analysis contributes anything to biblical scholarship is a question related to the broader issue of Lévi-Strauss's view of the structure of reality.

Paul Beauchamp on Gen 1. We turn to the work of an OT professor who is also at home in French structuralist thought. While Paul Beauchamp's *Création et séparation*[88] owes a great deal to the literary methodology of his Rome teacher Luis Alonso-Schökel, reviewers have rightly discerned its affinities to that of Lévi-Strauss in its emphasis on the opposites of unity and separation. But here the similarity to Leach's work ends. Beauchamp's lengthy first chapter is devoted to the surface structure (called by the author the "literary composition") of Gen 1, in which the ten words and the seven days of creation form a framework for discussion of various themes — particularly that of separation — in a variety of contexts. While the analysis contains overtones of subjectivity in its widespread discovery of the motif (even in Gen 1), the theme is never pressed as a key to the structure of reality.

Nor is Beauchamp uncomfortable with questions of a diachronic nature. In chap. 4 he attempts to find not merely a sociological but a historical milieu for Gen 1, and if his conclusion that it relates to the milieu of the Chronicler is not fully satisfactory other material in the work is a great deal more so. Upon finishing the book one feels that this great foundational chapter has itself been the object of study. In a manner not entirely unlike that of Umberto Cassuto, Beauchamp puts the emphasis back on the text, on its own internal structure, and on the meaning it conveys.

Recent Approaches

J. P. Fokkelman. By now it will be clear that no single approach to a biblical text can be called "structural" (as distinguished from "structuralistic") exegesis, but to round out this survey of related pentateuchal studies at least two recent works should be noted. J. P. Fokkelman's *Narrative Art in Genesis*[89] opens

87. Ibid.
88. Paul Beauchamp, *Création et séparation* (Paris: Aubier-Montaigne, 1969).
89. See n. 65 above.

with a helpful preface which explains both presuppositions and method. "Narrative art" is the key to interpretation because it was the key to composition, even in texts with both a religious and a historical base. Diachronic study at least works with a known entity, the text as received and read. By means of what is called a "stylistic and structural analysis," that is, the perceiving of the text as an organism or a literary work of art, one can derive both literary and theological conclusions.[90]

Fokkelman's purpose in the book is at least in part to demonstrate a certain methodology, a methodology which owes more to Alonso-Schökel than to any other scholar. The key word is style. Leaving aside all questions of development, the author studies two of the "smallest literary units" (the Tower of Babel, Gen 11:1-9; Jacob at Bethel, Gen 28:10-22), and then examines an "extended complex of about fifteen scenes" (the Jacob Cycle, Gen 25– 35).[91]

In the Tower of Babel story, the key to the narrator's art is found in the pun on "Babel" in v. 9. This wordplay is seen as "a gate to the story and primarily to its sound stratum."[92] Furthermore, Gen 11:1-9 "occupies a special position in OT narrative art by the density of its stylistically relevant phonological phenomena which are closely connected or coincide with remarkable verbal repetitions."[93] With the direction thus set, Fokkelman finds paronomasia (wordplay), alliteration, and various kinds of structural symmetry and reciprocity. In fact, two competing symmetries are observed, one parallel and one concentric. In the hands of Barthes, this might have provided the basis for an elaboration of the phenomena of universal conflict and ambiguity, but Fokkelman develops the meaning in another direction. In the *parallel* symmetry,[94] men (a) by their natural unity, (b) lay a plan, (c) set to building, (d) desiring to make a name, and (e) hope to avert a dispersion. In a parallel way, God (a) observes their unity, (b) thwarts their plan by His own, (c) to the abandonment of the building, (d) resulting in an anti-name and (e) dispersion. The *concentric* symmetry[95] is composed of six

90. Fokkelman, *Narrative Art*, p. 9.
91. Ibid., p. 85.
92. Ibid., p. 13.
93. Ibid.
94. Adapted from Fokkelman, pp. 20-21.
95. Adapted from Fokkelman, pp. 22-23.

pairs, with a turning point at the divine intervention of v. 7.

This illustration of the human confronting the divine in a paradigmatic way, as shown by the double schema, provides the beginning of a biblical theology in miniature. The author is teaching (note the element of intentionality) his readers a lesson: the tower builders at Babel are bad examples. The story is of crime and punishment, *hubris* and *nemesis*, a balance between man and God.[96] A stylistic analysis which exposes the basic forms of symmetry and the use of phonological phenomena here provides the key to meaning. Form has communicated content. The meaning contributes to the message.[97]

G. W. Coats. Turning to a second study in Genesis, *From Canaan to Egypt: Structural and Theological Context for the Joseph Story,*[98] by George W. Coats, we find both similarities to and differences from Fokkelman's work. Coats is much more evidently a form critic, for part of his task is to settle by structural means the question of sources in Gen 37–47. But his approach is literary, and his first chapter, upon which the final two are built, is an extended study of the literary features of the story. Here too symmetry is an important feature, although the building blocks are generally much more extended than the short phrases or individual words with which Fokkelman works. The story "as it was preserved in the MT [Masoretic Text]"[99] is assumed as an object of study, and questions of plot and development are asked of the whole. After demonstrating the structure and development of a unified plot, Coats concludes that, whatever its antecedents, the present expanded story is the product of a literary artisan, probably (as was argued by von Rad) from the era of Solomon.[100] Another chapter brings together questions of meaning, drawing on the structural studies of the opening chapter to some extent, but much more dependent than Fokkelman on resolving questions of historical setting and function.

---

96. Ibid., pp. 40-42.
97. The remainder of Fokkelman's book is written in a similar vein, though it places more emphasis on the context than I have been able to show in the examples cited.
98. See n. 65 above.
99. Coats, *From Egypt*, p. 7.
100. Ibid., pp. 77-79; von Rad, *Genesis*, pp. 434-35.

SUMMARY AND CONCLUSIONS

By way of critique there are many questions we might ask, but I would like to concentrate on a few of the basic hermeneutical issues raised by our examination and bypass for the moment some important secondary questions of method. I would like first to clarify what we mean by structural analysis, and then, using the definitions arrived at, review problems of meaning raised by the various definitions.

What is Structural Exegesis?

That the terminology of literary methodology requires a certain amount of sharpening must surely be apparent. In its strictest definition, structural analysis is that form of textual or exegetical work performed by the structuralist. Structuralists are those linguists, anthropologists, and litterateurs whose view of reality is defined by what is called structuralism. There may be various ways of understanding what structures lie at the heart of reality, but all structuralists are committed to the view that such structures exist. I would suggest that the term "structural analysis" be restricted for the sake of clarity to the methods employed by the structuralist proper.

Whether this will ever happen I do not know. Unfortunately, the term is currently applied in a broader sense to any research where the interest is synchronic rather than diachronic. Both "rhetorical criticism" and "literary criticism" have been suggested as alternative designations. But Culley argues for a distinction between *any* form of structural analysis on the one hand and rhetorical criticism on the other, based on whether the analysis limits itself to matters of style or explores other kinds of patterns.[101] It would appear that he sees the other patterns as the so-called deep levels of structure, and, whatever the case, his argument points out a distinction which surely cannot be overlooked. In addition, "literary" criticism has other connotations, as Gene Tucker has pointed out,[102] and to have two separate books in the Fortress Guide series dealing with two different topics yet titled with variations of the term "literary criticism"

---

101. Culley, "Structural Analysis," p. 169.
102. Tucker, in the Editor's Foreword to David Robertson, *The Old Testament and the Literary Critic*, p. viii.

borders on the ludicrous. Perhaps "style criticism" or "rhetorical criticism" might best describe that concern for stylistic research which does not build on French structuralism. In any case, the mixing of terminology is unhelpful. True structuralism is a comprehensive, antihistorical way of looking at reality, and structuralists like Paul Ricoeur have rightly questioned the mixture of historico-literary criticism and structural analysis that is increasing in some biblical study circles.[103]

Structural Analysis and the Quest for Meaning

Perhaps the most important questions involve the basic challenges which structuralism puts to us in the area of meaning. In the works of men like Polzin and Culley, I sense a willingness to experiment with structuralist method while retaining a certain ambivalence toward its claim to uncover ultimate meaning. It may be helpful to look again at the claims made for structural methods in this area, comparing them with historicist and evangelical hermeneutics. I must confess here to having no expertise in epistemological debate, but a study of structuralism presses one to some kind of response.

Structuralism. Meaning is found in the universal structures of reality. On the cover of a book of essays titled *Structural Analysis and Biblical Exegesis* there is a quote from Georges Crespy:

In the beginning was the structure. It was everywhere in the world and the world was organized by it.

It was in the minerals, in the crystals which always showed the same arrangement of their facets.

It was in the plant kingdom where the leaves are distributed along the stems and the veins along the leaves with an invariable regularity.

It was in the animal kingdom where physiological systems are connected to one another according to a schematic diagram whose program was determined in the gametes.

It was in the rhetoric, skilled in decomposing the discourse into its parts.[104]

103. Paul Ricoeur, "Biblical Hermeneutics," *Semeia* 4 (1975):29.
104. See n. 11 above.

Here is where the structuralist seeks meaning. The statement as we have it, however, has been historicized along lines familiar enough to those who have read the prologue of the Gospel of John. But is the structure a fact of history, a discoverable feature of what Christians understand to be the world? Is Crespy's attempt to place the structure in a historical setting, that is, to postulate a beginning, an element alien to the system? Structuralism does not see history as the realm of the meaningful. It looks rather for "the universal human mind,"[105] and this category, it has been argued, is antihistorical by nature.[106] The true structuralist is quite clear on this, and his analysis of a text does not seek the setting or intent; these must, in fact, be set aside to get at the deep structures, the universals which make up the myth. It seems that most biblical scholars who are attracted to structuralism have not been sufficiently willing to face this claim, though structuralists from Lévi-Strauss to Ricoeur have repeated it. Unless the Bible is to be seen as (mere) myth, rather than a record of the unique redemptive acts of God in the history of a particular people, I am not sure that the hermeneutical structures of the new analysis even apply. At this level I question whether there is any use for the method in evangelical biblical research.

Historicism. Meaning is to be found at the level of the original text, though it may not be accurate to suggest that there is any developed hermeneutical scheme attached to traditional historico-critical methods. In fact, the questions of ultimate meaning are often set aside, and perhaps this is one of the reasons for the current openness to a new methodology. But surely behind this kind of rigid historicism of much contemporary scholarship (if such a loaded term may be permitted) a set of hermeneutical assumptions is operating. Heir both to the Reformation and the Enlightenment, today's "Protestant literalism"[107] has assumed that the meaning of a given text is to be found in what its author intended to say, given an understanding of his historical, cultural, and linguistic milieu. The meaning is in a sense univocal; the key

---

105. Spivey, "Structuralism and Biblical Studies," p. 143.
106. Ibid., pp. 143-45.
107. Norman Brown, *Love's Body* (New York: Random House, Vintage Books, 1968), p. 212; cited in Spivey, "Structuralism and Biblical Studies," p. 143.

to unlocking it lies in a historically based, scientific study. It was left to the theologian to say whether what it meant at that time had any meaning for us today. The difficulty of this task may be appraised by looking at the exposition section in contrast to the exegetical notes of *The Interpreter's Bible*.[108] Source and form criticism add yet another problem: do we have in the text of the OT the authentic or earliest form of the writing or utterance? Implicit in these disciplines is the idea that earlier forms of the text are at least as meaningful as later forms, if not more so.

To such a situation structuralism or structuralist activity affords new possibilities.[109] The historically determined, univocal meaning, the meaning of the Sender, to use the structuralist term, has become oppressive. The discovery of symbol, the promise of meaning at a level other than the obvious, the role of the Receiver as well as the Sender, all these offer hope for new kinds of meaning. Norman Brown has called it "the end of the Protestant era, the end of Protestant literalism."[110]

Theological hermeneutics. If we are uncomfortable with the vague promises and alien philosophies of structuralism, perhaps we should be equally so with the historicist option, though for different reasons. The former reduces meaning to a set of structural absolutes known only to certain philosophers and in many instances at variance with the unique role of Scripture as a witness to God's *unusual* structure of reality. But historicism, by separating questions of meaning from literary research, has also lost a vital dimension. I would like to suggest a historical-literary-theological analysis as a valid corrective. Certainly evangelical scholarship cannot cut itself loose from what the text meant in a given space and time, for the historical nature of the faith requires this dimension. However, as J. P. Fokkelman, Robert Polzin, Paul Beauchamp, and others have shown, the literary structure of the text has often been ignored. This structure, no

108. Brevard S. Childs (*Biblical Theology in Crisis* [Philadelphia: Westminster Press, 1970], pp. 142-43) cites as an example the treatment of Gen 37:24 by C. A. Simpson and W. R. Bowie, "The Book of Genesis," in *The Interpreter's Bible* (New York: Abingdon Press, 1952), 1:754.

109. Spivey, "Structuralism and Biblical Studies," p. 143; Barr, *Bible in the Modern World*, pp. 64-65.

110. Norman Brown, *Love's Body*, p. 212; quoted by Spivey, "Structuralism and Biblical Studies," p. 143.

less than the historical setting, may be a conveyor of meaning. We have lost something by focusing on the author rather than the text. This kind of literary analysis (in contrast to structuralism or the antihistorical analysis of some literary scholars) carries with it no antihistorical philosophical baggage. A theological exegesis will set the historical-literary analysis in a framework of both biblical and historical theology. A diachronic study of the setting and sources of the text, supplemented by synchronic research into its structure and form, must then be followed by further diachronic examination. The text must be seen in its posthistory as well.

For an OT text this naturally includes the whole range of biblical theology, but I would like to suggest a further dimension. Brevard Childs has recently revived for a Protestant audience the science of tradition, that is, the history of the use of a given text in church and synagogue.[111] I know this is a rather un-Reformed thing to say, but I would suggest that we might benefit more from this kind of backward look than we sometimes gain from the more inward reflections of current semiology.

Conclusion

There is much that is attractive about the new semiology, particularly to evangelicals who have often felt attacked by the rationalistic historicism of OT scholarship since Wellhausen. But I would remind you: we have a great concern about and vested interest in history as the arena of God's redeeming activity. If we are attracted to structuralist exegesis at all, let us be so for the right reasons. It is not simply a handy way to circumvent documentary hypotheses but rather an entire system of hermeneutics. Our response, no less than the structuralist challenge, must address this larger issue.

---

111. Childs, *Biblical Theology in Crisis*, pp. 164-83; idem, *The Book of Exodus: A Critical, Theological Commentary*, Old Testament Library (Philadelphia: Westminister Press, 1974), pp. 20-26, 33-46, 80-89, etc.

V

Text Criticism

INTRODUCTION

A common assumption is that the text we are reading, whether ancient or modern, is what the author wrote. But even modern authors accept editorial changes or publisher's alterations as a valid and necessary part of seeing their labor through to its printed state. In the case of a book, letter, or article passed on from generation to generation, particularly before the days of mechanical reproduction, the possibility for textual change was all the greater. Of course, this is precisely the situation with respect to our manuscripts of the OT — the original author or authors wrote (or spoke) the message, and it was disseminated by means of hand copies from its beginning until the invention of moveable type in the time of Johannes Gutenberg (c. 1397-1468).

The earlier process inevitably gave rise over the years to a number of variant readings, and the science of "lower" or textual criticism developed as a way systematically to ascertain as nearly as possible what was written in the original text. Over 150 years of modern research have seen the development of highly sophisticated techniques practiced by both OT and NT specialists who work on almost nothing but the matter of text. In this field there has been little concern for theological position, and conservative critics generally take their place alongside those of other theological persuasions.

Of course, to a person with a high view of scriptural authority and its truth-value, concern for a proper text should naturally follow. If the Bible is God's Word in the words of prophets and apostles, clearly there must be more than a passing interest in its correct transmission. If a text is to provide the means of teaching, reproving, correcting, and training in the faith, then its readers must have confidence that what they are reading is what God intended them to have.

The science of text criticism must work differently for each Testament. In NT studies the task is largely a matter of comparing and weighing a considerable number of ancient manuscripts (MSS; sing. MS). The various NT documents were completed by A.D. 100, so the period of composition was relatively short. By the mid-second century numerous copies of many books were circulating, and we have MS evidence for such copies beginning with the small fragment of John 18 (Rylands Papyrus 52) that dates to the first half of the second century. With the development of the codex (book form) c. A.D. 200 a more stable means of circulating connected MSS became popular, and major extant NT codices reach back to the early fourth century A.D. Thus NT text criticism is rich with comparative material, much of which is relatively close in time to its source.

In OT studies the MS situation is entirely different. Until 1947 the oldest complete texts of the Hebrew Bible were in four extant copies of the ben Asher or Masoretic Bible, of which the earliest (the Cairo Codex) has been dated to the late ninth century A.D. This Masoretic text (MT) itself represented a long tradition of Jewish text criticism and unfortunately led to the destruction of other MSS. With the discovery of the Dead Sea Scrolls in 1947, the text critic's MS evidence for some portions of the OT went backward from c. A.D. 1000 to before the time of Christ, but the number of texts available for comparison is still very limited. For this reason OT text critics have often resorted to a consideration of the ancient versions (VSS; sing. VS), which are translations made in the years before the MT was standardized. The Greek VS called the Septuagint (LXX), which was produced by Alexandrian Jewry and part of which dates from as early as the mid-third century B.C., is of course the most valuable witness. Behind this text scholars have often been able to discern a Hebrew original differing in certain respects from the MT and also from the Dead Sea Scrolls.

Other unique features of the OT make it difficult to speak of a correct text in NT terms. Perhaps basic to all is the question of composition. While the job of the text critic is to work back to the original writings or "autographs," it is not clear in the case of many OT books that there was an original autograph in the sense that there was an original letter to the Galatians written by Paul or his secretary. With a letter by Paul we can trace the history of errors or changes, grouping the available MSS into families[1] and evaluating the texts by standard rules. In contrast, books like Jeremiah and 1 Samuel seem to have come together over a period of time with additions or corrections to the text being made during the period of fluidity. Comparisons of the MT with the LXX show that the matter is far more complex than one might imagine, with the result that the job of the text critic overlaps the work of the literary and form critic to some extent.

At this point the question naturally arises, "What stage of the text represents the inspired Word of God?" To this there is no simple answer, but we need not be unduly disturbed. Two main textual traditions claim our attention, the one embodied in a Jewish Hebrew text from c. A.D. 1100 (i.e., the MT), and the other the Hebrew from which the LXX was produced. While there are many distinct differences, few if any present doctrinal difficulties and Christians have at various times used both as Scripture. It is the final form of the text as handed down to us in which first Jewish and then Christian believers found their source of spiritual truth. If more light is cast on either the process of composition or the history of textual transmission, this can only establish more firmly the text accepted by synagogue and church, and although some uncertainty might remain regarding what has been traditionally called an autograph, we can have confidence that at some point the people of God saw in our text that which they recognized to be the sovereign Word of God.

The "original text," then, for the OT student, is the canonical text; that is to say, at whatever stage the believing community settled upon a particular book or collection of books as inspired, they had, and we have, the Word of God. In this way inspiration is seen as applying to the end product of what was in some cases a long process, while the length of the process in no way affects its authority. But since most if not all of our OT books were accepted as canonical well before any of the MSS which we possess were made, the task of the text critic is to determine the

---

1. Groups of MSS that descended (were copied) from a given early MS, thus incorporating all of its peculiarities.

oldest or most likely original reading among the options now available.

A relatively new science has risen to challenge the OT text critic proper. Whereas in former years it was the practice to look for an alternate text to resolve a difficulty in reading, now many scholars go first to cognate (related) languages. The science of comparative philology, as the discipline is called, seeks to find its clues in a forgotten meaning for an obscure word or phrase rather than in an error of writing or copying. Thus many of the difficulties which were called textual problems in an earlier day are now seen as philological (linguistic) problems; there was nothing wrong with the text—we simply did not know what it meant![2]

We have now seen some of the problems and the range of possibilities. A treatment such as this can necessarily only skim the surface, and the discipline of text criticism is properly the work of experts.[3] But an awareness of the issues and methods will help students of the OT to find their way through the maze of sometimes conflicting claims that are made. We have a reasonably good knowledge of the subject, at least as far as the layperson's need to establish what his Bible says is concerned, though this should never lead to complacency.

DEVELOPMENT OF THE OLD TESTAMENT TEXT

Early Period

Text and canon. According to traditional dating, all the OT books were completed by the time of Ezra at a gathering which talmudic sages called the Great Synagogue or Great Assembly, sometime around the middle of the fifth century B.C.[4] Prior to that time, and indeed for over a hundred years afterward, there is little to discuss by way of text criticism, for, whatever the actual state of the text of any given book of the Bible, MS evidence is

2. For a description and careful evaluation, see James Barr, *Comparative Philology and the Text of the Old Testament* (Oxford: At the Clarendon Press, 1968).
3. For those who wish a fuller treatment of the subject some fine introductions are available, particularly by Bleddyn J. Roberts, *The Old Testament Text and Versions* (Cardiff: University of Wales Press, 1951); Ernst Würthwein, *The Text of the Old Testament*, 4th ed. trans. Errol F. Rhodes (Grand Rapids: Eerdmans, 1979). For additional bibliography, any good Bible dictionary may be consulted.
4. Babylonian Talmud *Baba Bathra* 14b, 15a. (Allowance was made for later genealogies in Chronicles.)

completely lacking. We may assume for some books a fully fixed form and for others a fluid tradition well into the Persian period (c. 538-332 B.C.), but details must be left to speculation.

There is no reason, however, why this state of affairs should raise skepticism about the reliability of our text; what we know about copying methods as well as attitudes to sacred books leads rather to confidence in its careful preservation. By the time of Ezra writing had been common in the ancient Near East for 2000 years, and the role of the scribe was known in some form in Israel itself from the days of the Judges.[5] The figure of the *sōpēr* or scribe in Judg 5:14 seems more analogous to a kind of muster official, a usage which identifies the scribe with counting rather than writing. Thus it is not so strange that Babylonian Talmud *Qiddushin* 30a tells of the later *sōpĕrîm* (scribes) who in the four centuries after Ezra copied out verses of the Torah (law), even counting the letters so as to avoid unintentional error.[6] While such traditions as that of *Qiddushin* 30a come from a much later period (third century A.D. or after), there is little reason to doubt that they reflect a careful attitude to Scripture in earlier Jewish scribal circles.

But what was considered Scripture in this period? As might be expected, the time from Ezra through to the first Christian century was also the time when the Jewish list or canon of books became well established. Moreover, the development of an authoritative text is a natural corollary to an authoritative list of books. Both movements probably received impetus from a realization that the Jewish community was becoming increasingly scattered geographically and diverse culturally. Aramaic, which was the language of the synagogue as it developed in the Babylonian Exile, did not pose a direct threat to the sacred Hebrew tongue, and parts of Ezra and Daniel are actually written in Aramaic. Nevertheless, as Hebrew became less and less the language of the working Jew in both Palestine and the Dispersion,

5. Cf. Judg 5:14, literally "those who wield the rod of the scribe." Whether these early scribes were copyists is doubtful, but by the time of Ezra the office was well developed and involved guarding or teaching the law as well as transmitting sacred writings (Ezra 7:6).
6. See M. H. Segal, "The Promulgation of the Authoritative Text of the Hebrew Bible," in *The Canon and Masorah of the Hebrew Bible: An Introductory Reader*, ed. Sid Z. Leiman, Library of Biblical Studies (New York: Ktav Publishing House, 1974), p. 288. (Reprinted from *Journal of Biblical Literature* 72 [1953]:35-47.)

and as the synagogue became the focal point of Jewish life, some provision for transmitting the Scriptures to the common person became increasingly necessary. The answer to the need, as traced back from later written sources, was a series of orally recited translations or paraphrases called Targums, many of which have since been preserved in writing. While the strongly interpretative nature of the Targums, as well as a lack of contemporary sources, makes it difficult to use targumic material for textual study, the situation does testify to the obvious fact that a standard Hebrew text would be seen as an asset to the community creating the Targums.[7]

A much greater challenge soon moved the Jewish community further toward a set canon and text. It came in the form of Hellenistic culture, which arose and dominated the eastern Mediterranean world following upon the victories of Alexander the Great in the late fourth century B.C. While details are scarce, there is evidence that both text and canon were discussed at length, and certain directions are clear. In the matter of canon, contemporary evidence from chaps. 44–50 of the Book of Jesus Son of Sirach (Ecclesiasticus), written c. 185 B.C., shows that the figures revered by the Jerusalem sage were largely those known in the present canonical books. The writer even uses a literary category like "the Twelve Prophets," the common Hebrew name for the minor prophets. Writing a preface to his translation of Ecclesiasticus into Greek, Sirach's grandson in 132 B.C. even classifies the sacred books into the now familiar division of "the law and the prophets and the other books of our fathers" (cf. also Luke 24:44). None of this can answer explicitly the question of when and how the concept of canon came to be applied, but it was plainly an emerging and necessary movement. By NT times the number and names of the books were fairly well settled, and neither the Jews nor the early church entertained serious doubts about the subject.[8] At the end of the first Christian century, Josephus could number the books of the Hebrew Bible with no significant fear of contradiction.[9]

---

7. See further John Bowker, *The Targums and Rabbinic Literature: An Introduction to Jewish Interpretations of Scripture* (Cambridge: At the University Press, 1969).

8. See Sid Z. Leiman, *The Canonization of Hebrew Scripture: The Talmudic and Midrashic Evidence* (Hamden, Conn.: Archon Books, 1976).

9. Josephus, *Contra Apion*, 1.37-43.

Textual standardization. Accompanying this formation of the canon within the Greek period, and for our purposes more to the point, were moves toward standardization of the text. Again, the impetus may have come from a wide cultural spread that was increasingly separating the hellenized Jews of the Dispersion from the traditional learning of Palestine, and certainly the separation gave rise to what is perhaps our earliest witness to the OT text — the Septuagint (LXX), a Greek translation of the OT.

Greek language and culture, unlike Aramaic, did not easily accommodate itself to Jewish learning. Moreover, Alexander and some of his successors in the Ptolemaic and Seleucid kingdoms pursued an open policy of cultural as well as military conquest, a movement which threatened the integrity of groups like the Jews throughout the empire. If hellenization had fully succeeded in its objectives, it is doubtful that any Judaism as we know it would have remained from Roman times onward. But as often happens, a measure of accommodation was reached, with the result that a translation of the Bible into the new language was requested. According to the partially fictitious Letter of Aristeas, King Ptolemy II Philadelphus (285-246 B.C.) commissioned a translation of the Bible into Greek for use by the Jews in Alexandria. Although few if any contemporary scholars believe that the resulting LXX VS was completed during Ptolemy's reign, it was then that work on this VS probably began.

A text of the original is presupposed by every translation. While no direct evidence for an authoritative Hebrew text is extant for this period, the LXX shows certain tendencies which must have marked the Hebrew text or texts used by its various translators. For many years considered by scholars the product of an inferior Hebrew text, the LXX has now received new attention in the light of comparison with the Dead Sea Scrolls.[10] At the same time, however, the LXX shows enough evidence of variety in textual matters to caution against positing a too static textual situation in the years when it was being produced. In any case, its very presence and use as the Bible of an increasingly large segment of the Jewish world must have had the effect of

---

10. For a somewhat controversial and perhaps overly optimistic assessment, see Ralph W. Klein, *Textual Criticism of the Old Testament: The Septuagint after Qumran*, Guides to Biblical Scholarship, Old Testament Series (Philadelphia: Fortress Press, 1974).

either making the LXX text a new standard, or of making the Jews decide what was to be considered an authoritative Hebrew text.

Discovery of the Dead Sea Scrolls (DSS) at Qumran in 1947 gave the modern situation an entirely new dimension. The scrolls from Qumran give no direct evidence for one set text or canon, but they provide abundant inferential evidence concerning the state of both. Although the Qumran monastics were a breakaway sectarian group, they did not use a Bible any different from that of the Jews in Jerusalem and Alexandria. Nor did their text or texts — for there is evidence of variety — necessarily exhibit sectarian tendencies; they simply show more variety than one might have expected in strict circles.

Whether to explain the variety as a direct result of the peculiar place of the Essenes in the Judaism of the period, or to see in it a reflection of the normal situation, is still an issue of debate.[11] It has even been argued that during the period in question (c. 130 B.C. – A.D. 68) there emerged a standard text, a *textus receptus*,[12] though general opinion holds that the evidence points not to emergence of a standard text but rather to a variety of textual families, at least in Qumran, right to the end.[13] Frank M. Cross, perhaps with an eye to NT models, posits the existence of three such families and suggests that they developed between the fifth and first centuries B.C., "in Palestine, in Egypt, and in a third locality, presumably Babylon";[14] not only the Qumran scrolls, he argues, but the LXX and the MT incorporate elements of all three traditions, and various complex relationships between the three may be discerned.[15] What is clear is that the variety of texts available does not seem to have particularly bothered the

11. See Shemaryahu Talmon, "The Old Testament Text," in *The Cambridge History of the Bible*, vol. 1, *From the Beginnings to Jerome*, ed. P. R. Ackroyd and C. F. Evans (Cambridge: At the University Press, 1970), pp. 184-86; Bleddyn J. Roberts, "The Old Testament: Manuscripts, Text, and Versions," in *The Cambridge History of the Bible*, vol. 2, *The West from the Fathers to the Reformation*, ed. G. W. H. Lampe (1969), pp. 2-4.

12. Segal, "Promulgation of the Authoritative Text," pp. 285-86, 295.

13. Talmon, "The OT Text," p. 186.

14. Frank M. Cross, Jr., "The Contribution of the Qumran Discoveries to the Study of the Biblical Text," in *Canon and Masorah*, p. 339. (Reprinted from *Israel Exploration Journal* 16 [1966]:81-95.)

15. For a chart of Cross's view of these relationships see Talmon, "The OT Text," p. 195.

Qumran covenanters; there is no evidence that they tried to eliminate any of them or "correct" the readings they found. But whether such fluidity also existed in Jerusalem circles is another and more important question.

A further witness, doubtless from this period though preserved in later copies, is what is known today as the Samaritan Pentateuch (SP). According to Cross and his students, the SP arose directly from the original Palestinian Hebrew text type and reflects a split from other traditions connected with the Samaritan schism, the date of which they have lowered to the first century B.C. when the Hasmonean king John Hyrcanus attacked Shechem.[16] The Samaritan tradition, if it can be thus placed in a historical framework, takes its place as a witness to an early recension of the text.

So in view of this general situation we must ask again: what is the evidence for a textual standardization, and when does it appear? If the materials discovered at Qumran leave the matter in doubt, what other evidence is there?

At this point we return to traditions emanating from what became the normative group within Judaism, the rabbinic academies which arose after the destruction of the temple in A.D. 70. According to all their sources, these so-called Tannaim (rabbis who flourished from A.D. 10 until the Mishnah was published c. A.D. 200) were bound in textual matters to the Masorah, that is, traditions representing the text, its exact makeup, and any peculiarities it contained.[17] While the tradition of a fixed text goes back in rabbinic sources to the period prior to A.D. 70, the matter becomes more precise with quotations from the famous Rabbi Akiba (c. A.D. 55-137) whose commitment to an authoritative text is quite unambiguous.[18] In addition to the talmudic citations, we now have more direct indications of the standardization of the proto-Masoretic text type in fragments of biblical MSS from the Jewish revolt of A.D. 132-135, during which Akiba supported the pretended messiah Bar Kochba. Texts from both

16. Frank M. Cross, Jr., "Aspects of Samaritan and Jewish History in Late Persian and Hellenistic Times," *Harvard Theological Review* 59 (1966):201-11; James D. Purvis, *The Samaritan Pentateuch and the Origin of the Samaritan Sect*, Harvard Semitic Monographs 2 (Cambridge: Harvard University Press, 1969); Klein, *Textual Criticism of the OT*, p. 18.

17. Roberts, *OT Text and Versions*, pp. 40-45.

18. Roberts, "Manuscripts, Text, and Versions," pp. 1-2.

Masada and nearby Murabba'at conform in substantial respects to what became the Masoretic tradition,[19] the ancestor of the text used in all Hebrew Bibles from the Middle Ages to the present. (Recent attempts to show variety within the Masoretic tradition do not affect the basic point.)[20] We are left with clear evidence for a fixed textual tradition in the early second century A.D, at least among those whose influence predominated among subsequent generations of Jewish scholars.

A final area of textual spadework is found in the numerous biblical passages quoted in the NT, and here there is little evidence for a standard text. Even a writer like Paul, for whom the LXX provides the major source of quotations,[21] shows no uniformity of practice; his quotations even exhibit considerable variety in distribution among LXX text forms. Of the remaining (i.e., non-LXX) quotations, some seem to use a Hebrew text while others may employ an Aramaic Targum, a different Greek translation, or a free quotation from memory, such that the question of the extent to which NT writers, like targumic rabbis, used "a free rendering in accordance with literary custom or for an exegetical purpose" has occupied NT scholars extensively in recent years.[22] In short, the evidence of the NT does not lend itself to being used for working back to an authoritative Hebrew text.

Summary. The question which remains, therefore, is how far back the idea of a standardized text can be traced. Do we take the evidence from Qumran with its fluidity of traditions as representing a situation that also obtained in the more orthodox circles of Jerusalem Judaism down to the time of Christ? Or do

19. Ibid., p. 2; also Moshe Greenberg, "The Stabilization of the Text of the Hebrew Bible, Reviewed in the Light of the Biblical Materials from the Judean Desert," in *Canon and Masorah*, pp. 298-326, esp. 316-17. (Reprinted from *Journal of the American Oriental Society* 76 [1956]:157-67.)

20. E.g., Harry M. Orlinsky, "The Masoretic Text: A Critical Evaluation," Prolegomenon to reprinted ed. of Christian D. Ginsburg, *Introduction to the Massoretico-Critical Edition of the Hebrew Bible* (1897; reprint ed. New York: Ktav Publishing House, 1966). (Reprinted in *Canon and Masorah*, pp. 833-77.)

21. Of 93 citations 51 are found in virtual agreement with the LXX, according to E. Earle Ellis, *Paul's Use of the Old Testament* (Edinburgh: Oliver and Boyd, 1957), pp. 11-12 and Appendix I (A).

22. Ibid., p. 14. See also M. P. Miller, "Targum, Midrash, and the Use of the Old Testament in the New Testament," *Journal for the Study of Judaism* 2 (1971):29-82; M. J. McNamara, "Targums," *Interpreter's Dictionary of the Bible,* Supplementary Volume (Nashville: Abingdon Press, 1976), pp. 856-61 and bibliography.

we accept the evidence of rabbinic traditions concerning pre-Christian *sōperîm* and their work, and about the care with which Jews of old guarded their text?[23] The layperson, whatever his theological persuasion, must look to specialists for the answers to such questions, and unfortunately the experts do not agree. Again it should be remembered that (1) the variations in text represented by all traditions are not such that any basic doctrine is affected, and (2) the science of OT text criticism is still young. There exists a good possibility that additional scrolls may yet be found which will help to unravel some of these perplexing questions.

That inspired apostles and our Lord Himself were able to find the Word of God in a variety of texts should caution us against undue skepticism if we fail to reach agreement. At the same time, the high regard in which they held the Scriptures drives us to consider the proper text important, and evangelical scholars must join with others in sifting and evaluating the materials now extant.

Masoretic Period

Masorah. The state of the text is better known for the period of A.D. 220 to the Middle Ages, a period of intense and fruitful activity in Jewish circles. The "masorah" — traditions and details regarding the text — were codified and eventually written into the margins of biblical MSS, probably by the late fifth century A.D.[24] These data effectively built the "fence around the law" of which Akiba spoke, and helped the copyist to eliminate almost every semblance of error. (Those rabbis who produced the Masorah — also spelled Massorah — became known as Masoretes; hence Masoretic Text or MT.) Selected results of these labors are incorporated into the margin of *Biblia Hebraica* (3d ed. 1937 onward), but since most of these notations establish or record some fact about an already standardized text rather than give the evidence of other MSS or VSS, they are of little use to the average student in making text-critical decisions.[25]

---

23. Segal, "Promulgation of the Authoritative Text," p. 288; Josephus, *Contra Apion*, 1.8, 42.

24. See Roberts, *OT Text and Versions*, chaps. 3–4.

25. A helpful introduction to their meaning can be found in Würthwein, *Text of the OT*, pp. 15-29.

Vocalization. A second result of rabbinic activity during the Masoretic period was the addition to the text of a system of vowels. Ancient Hebrew was first written in a script which recorded only the consonants, a defect which created substantial problems when the language was no longer well known. At some point in the early period texts began to include the weak consonants *aleph, he, waw,* and *yodh* to act as vowels in strategic places where ambiguity was the greatest. Known as *matres lectionis* ("mothers of reading"), these consonants acting as vowels effectively settled the pronunciation and hence the meaning of ambiguous forms. The *matres,* however, were nevertheless intrusions into the sacred text and later some Masoretes objected as a matter of principle to their insertion. Thus it was inevitable that some kind of external vowel system would eventually be introduced to aid reading and to promote an approved or correct pronunciation. To meet the former requirement a transliteration of the Hebrew text was made into Greek letters (with vowels) some time before the third century A.D., and Origen incorporated it into the second column of his Hexapla. But something more was needed, especially since Jews were ill-disposed to use a Greek text. Probably, however, it was not until after the fifth century that our modern systems of "pointing," that is, of little signs for vowels placed above and below the line, were introduced. Of the three that are known — Babylonian, Palestinian, and Tiberian — the Tiberian system ultimately prevailed, probably under the influence of the celebrated Tiberian Masoretes ben Asher and ben Naphtali in the tenth century.

The implications of this history for textual study are immediately apparent. Not only is it difficult to be sure we have an authentic pronunciation, but there were manifold possibilities for errors in understanding. B. J. Roberts cites Jerome and Babylonian Talmud *Baba Bathra* 21ab to show that problems were recognized already in the earlier period. The three consonants *dbr* in Jer 9:21 could be read as *dābār,* "a word," *deber,* "pestilence," or *dabbēr,* "to speak"; while *zkr* in Deut 25:19 could be read as *zēker,* "remembrance," or *zākār,* "male."[26] Examples could be multiplied, and contemporary scholars differ greatly in the respect they accord the final vocalization of the rabbis. When we

26. Roberts, *OT Text and Versions,* p. 49.

remember that at least 700 years separate the standardization of the consonantal text from that of the vowel points, the relative authority of each becomes clearer. At the same time, as Würthwein rightly cautions, the Masoretic vowels were not the result of innovation but of attempts to record the tradition they had received, and should not be quickly dismissed;[27] whether commentaries like Mitchell Dahood's Anchor Bible *Psalms* have gone too far in this regard must be left to the reader to judge.[28] A glance at such volumes will show the range of possibilities, particularly in the light of recently recovered cognate languages, but the beginning student is well advised to proceed slowly.

Kethib-Qere. Another feature probably to be dated in the period A.D. 200-1200 is a device known as the *kethib-qere*. In about 1500 places, the MT has a variant word written into the margin (or sometimes unwritten but to be understood) for a word in the text. The word in the text, the *kethib* (what is "written"), obviously represents what the Masoretes considered to be authoritative from the standpoint of their textual tradition. But then, how do we explain the *qere* (what is "read") in the margin? If the rabbis thought the written text to be inviolate, why would they suggest a substitute reading?

This problem has long puzzled scholars, but some helpful studies have been produced in the present century.[29] First, the *qere*s are divided into groups on the basis of age and type. The oldest are seen as a substitution of the word *'ădōnāy* (Lord) for the four-letter name of God, the tetragrammaton *yhwh* which the Jews came to regard as too sacred too pronounce. The second stage is seen as a simple use of euphemism for circumventing offensive words in public reading,[30] and a third stage as an attempt to clarify ambiguous pronunciation in the absence of vowels. The last stage, it is now argued, represented not a correction of the text (which would have been unthinkable) but the evidence

27. Würthwein, *Text of the OT*, p. 27.

28. Mitchell Dahood, *Psalms I–III*, 3 vols., Anchor Bible 16, 17, 17A (Garden City, N.Y.: Doubleday & Company, 1965-1970).

29. See esp. Robert Gordis, *The Biblical Text in the Making: A Study of the Kethib-Qere*, augmented ed. with a prolegomenon (New York: Ktav Publishing House, 1971).

30. E.g., *dbywnym* ("dove's dung"?) for the possibly offensive form *ḥrywynym* or *ḥry ywnym* (also "dung of doves") in 2 Kgs 6:25.

of variant readings in MSS which lay before the Masoretes as they worked. This type would represent, for the modern textual scholar, not a later attempt to read sense into the text, but evidence of an otherwise forgotten reading from a MS which is now lost.

Ben Asher text. Finally, in the tenth century, under the influence of the two families of Tiberian Masoretes ben Asher and ben Naphtali, movement progressed toward a standard authoritative textual recension within the Masoretic tradition. This *textus receptus* which finally emerged triumphant was largely that of ben Asher,[31] and the resulting text which became standard for subsequent generations was complete with vowels, Masorah, and *kethib-qere* readings. Although the earliest MSS of the so-called ben Asher text are not as uniform as one might expect, it is with the acceptance of ben Asher in the twelfth century by the great rabbi Maimonides that the text becomes set.

Text sources. What sources do we have for the Masoretes and where does their influence show itself in our translations? Of ancient texts, a few have survived which claim actually to come from the ben Asher family itself, while others at least represent the period. Probably the oldest is a codex of the Prophets from a synagogue in Cairo, produced by Moshe ben Asher and dated A.D. 895. Of more importance because of its association with Maimonides is the Aleppo Codex, now partially recovered and in possession of the state of Israel after suffering some damage by fire in 1949. This MS, which dates from the early tenth century, serves as the basis for a new critical text of the OT currently under production by the Hebrew University in Jerusalem. A third major witness to the MT is the Leningrad Codex B 19a (frequently know as L), containing the entire OT and written in A.D. 1008. Claiming to have been copied directly from a text prepared by Aaron, son of Moshe ben Asher, it was used as the basis for the third or 1937 edition of *Biblia Hebraica* (frequently abbreviated as *BH³*) and for *Biblia Hebraica Stuttgartensia (BHS)*. Apart from these, a tenth-century MS in the British Museum

31. This although recent studies in MSS of the MT have shown that the matter is not a simple choice of one or the other; see, e.g., Paul Kahle, *The Cairo Geniza*, 2d ed. (Oxford: Basil Blackwell, 1959).

(Or 4445) and the Babylonian Codex of the Prophets (MS Heb. B 3) from Leningrad dated A.D. 916 make up the collection. Since none of these MSS was available to the translators of the European versions at the time of the Reformation, Bibles like the *Authorized* or *King James Version (AV, KJV)* are based on later and inferior evidence; their basic text, however, is clearly the MT. Of particular interest is the printed edition of Jacob ben Chayim's Second Rabbinic Bible, produced in 1525 by collating several MSS. Ben Chayim's critical text became the basis for almost all subsequent Bibles until modern times, and it is a direct ancestor of our pre-1937 English Bibles.

An additional source of Masoretic readings from before ben Asher came to light with the discovery of a vast collection of discarded books and MSS during the renovation of a Cairo synagogue in 1890. The history of the Geniza (discard room) and its treasure store is long and complex,[32] but suffice it to say that thousands of pieces of biblical MSS alone were found, and many of them date from or before the time of ben Asher. Here evidence is found for vocalization and text types from before the tenth century, a witness that no post-Maimonides MS could reliably provide.

Ancient versions. Finally, recourse may be made to textual evidence from translations which were made during the years under discussion. We have already mentioned the Septuagint, the Targums, and the Samaritan Pentateuch, all of which predate the standardizing of the Hebrew text during the early Christian era. The earliest VS to reflect the set text is another Greek Bible, the literal rendering of a second-century Greek Jew named Aquila who wished to provide a Greek Bible which would avoid the so-called Christian readings of the LXX: on the whole, his underlying text is like the MT. A Greek VS from later in the second century was rendered by Theodotion, and it appears to be a revision of the LXX employing a different type of MT; unlike Aquila's version, it seems to have been used chiefly by Christians. A slightly more interpretative Greek translation by Symmachus, also of the second century, is preserved in only a few fragments. Most of the remaining VSS from this period (including the Syriac Peshitta, Coptic, Ethiopic, Old Latin, and Vulgate) are generally

32. See Kahle, *The Cairo Geniza.*

dependent on texts we have already noted, and are rarely of major importance for making text-critical decisions.

HEBREW TEXTS AND ENGLISH VERSIONS

We have seen something of the materials available for scholars seeking to produce a critical edition of the OT. But what of the average pastor, teacher, or theological student, the person with only a basic knowledge of the language and no access to the British Museum or the Cairo Synagogue? Or even more to the point for most of us, what about the text which is used to translate our favorite English version? Is it pure Masoretic, mixed Masoretic, a conflation of Hebrew readings, a variety of Hebrew and evidence from the VSS, or (even) replete with conjectural reconstructions?

Hebrew Texts

Let us begin with the first question: what text is available to the Hebrew student and how can he determine its correctness? In most cases a choice is made by the instructor, who passes the word that only the compendious *Biblia Hebraica* (*BH³*, 1937)[33] will do. This Bible, formidable for reasons of size alone, was critically edited from the Leningrad Codex B 19a by Paul Kahle and a predominantly German team of scholars, and it rendered all pre-1937 Bibles obsolete. Alongside the text are printed the Masorah Parva, notes left by the rabbis to guard the external form of the text from corruption. And below the last line of text the student is confronted with two registers of notes. The upper register contains lists of variants, many of which were collated from late MSS by Bishop Benjamin Kennicott, J. B. de Rossi, and Christian D. Ginsburg. Together with these variants (which prove largely that all late MSS are fairly standard) are printed certain readings of lesser importance from non-Hebrew VSS. In a second and lower register of notes, those variants considered more probable or more important by the editors find their place. Important *kethib-qere* readings, together with vital evidence from the LXX, SP, and now also the DSS are included. An unfortunate char-

---

33. *Biblia Hebraica*, 3d ed. (Stuttgart: Württembergische Bibelanstalt, 1937). The previous editions (1906, 1912) were edited by Rudolph Kittel, and by custom the work often stands under his name, abbreviated as *BHK*.

acteristic was the inclusion of a large number of conjectural readings, but this shortcoming is now corrected to a great extent in the *Biblia Hebraica Stuttgartensia* edition (*BHS*, 1967-1977).[34] Nevertheless, for the average student, *BH³* is probably the place to begin. In *BH³* and *BHS* are produced a good, early ben Asher MT, together with a critical apparatus that contains most of the data required to make textual decisions. In the light of new material available since 1937, a fresh critical edition will hopefully emerge, but in the meantime *BH³* and *BHS* are still reliable tools.

Equally available and far less bulky is the British and Foreign Bible Society edition of the Hebrew Bible edited by Norman H. Snaith. This Bible, designed as a replacement for the older Letteris text, was based on certain Spanish MSS (chiefly Or 2626-28, executed in Lisbon c. 1482) which Snaith found in the British Museum and which reproduce in most respects the ben Asher text used by Kahle. Snaith included some of the official Masoretic notes but omitted the emendations and critical apparatus of *BH³*. The Snaith Bible is therefore a faithful copy of good MSS of the MT, but cannot itself be used for comparing textual evidence.

A new and valuable (though hardly pocket-sized) tool for the text critic has been promised with the publication of *The Book of Isaiah* (chaps. 1–22) of the Hebrew University Bible Project.[35] Based on the Aleppo Codex, it has an apparatus collecting variants from (1) the VSS, (2) the DSS and rabbinic literature (pre-Masoretic, representing the early period), (3) medieval Hebrew MSS (Masoretic), and (4) minor variants of spelling, vowels, and accents from early Masoretic texts. Its advantage in employing the Aleppo Codex as a basis, and its clear and judicious registering of the variants, will make the Hebrew University Bible a new standard. A full and invaluable introduction to the project has been published by chief editor M. H. Goshen-Gottstein in *The Book of Isaiah: Sample Edition with Introduction.*[36]

For textual purposes, any edition of the Hebrew Bible other than those described should be used with great care.

34. K. Elliger and W. Rudolph, eds., *Biblia Hebraica Stuttgartensia* (Stuttgart: Deutsche Bibelstiftung, 1967-1977).

35. Moshe H. Goshen-Gottstein, *The Book of Isaiah,* Parts One and Two, Hebrew University Bible Project (Jerusalem: Magnes Press, 1975).

36. M. H. Goshen-Gottstein, *The Book of Isaiah: Sample Edition with Introduction,* Hebrew University Bible Project (Jerusalem: Magnes Press, 1965).

English Versions

It is one thing to have a good Hebrew text and adequate tools for the text critic. But readers of English Bibles have the right to ask whether their versions also can be relied upon for faithful representation of the best text. We sometimes hear claims, especially from those who decry the use of newer versions, that the text has been tampered with; or, from the opposite side, we hear claims that all other Bibles are translated from obsolete texts. From the historical survey above it should be clear that newer translations have advantages from a textual standpoint, but what is not so immediately apparent is that even modern OT translations differ widely in the attitude toward the text which they employ.

This again is a point at which the OT differs from the NT. Since the days of Westcott and Hort, NT translations have followed some form of the eclectic text along lines worked out in the nineteenth century. On the other hand, with the OT the question is not one of selecting the best Masoretic MSS; editions of the Hebrew Bible since 1937 show remarkable uniformity. The question, rather, is how much weight to give to other witnesses (e.g., the VSS, the Targums, and the DSS), as well as how much conjecture to allow when none of the direct evidence can resolve a difficulty. These are the reasons why modern translations are in more general agreement on NT readings but show great variety in their handling of the OT. (Examples will be given below in the section dealing with textual problems.)

Nevertheless, the question of any translation's broader textual basis is also of interest. In general it can be said that the older Protestant translations (*KJV, English Revised, American Standard,* etc.) based their OT translation as far as possible on the ben Chayim *textus receptus* of 1525. Where difficulties were encountered, they were loath to resort to the VSS, a feeling summed up by the translators of the *KJV* in their preface. While defending early Christian use of an inferior VS like the LXX, they are of the opinion that "the translation of the *Seventie* dissenteth from the Originall in many places, neither doeth it come neere it, for perspicuitie, gravitie, maiestie. . . ." They further find that "it needed in many places correction," and that "the *Seventie* were Interpreters . . . sometimes they may be noted to adde to the Originall, and sometimes to take from it; which made the Apostles to leave them many times, when they left the *Hebrew*, and to deliver the sence thereof according to the trueth of the word, as the spirit gave them utterance. This may suffice touching the Greeke Translations of the old Testament."

While the above appears to be understandably unaware of modern textual issues, it does show the attitude of the translators in 1611 regarding textual correction from the VSS. The LXX is inferior not only because of its interpretative tendency but because its text is thought to expand or delete from what the learned divines unhesitatingly label the "Originall." They have no doubt but that in the Second Rabbinic Bible of Jacob ben Chayim they were handling the very Word of God. When they affirm that Hebrew and Greek are the "tongues wherein God was pleased to speake to his Church," they mean the *textus receptus* of their day: "Neither did wee thinke much to consult the Translators or Commentators, *Chaldee, Hebrewe, Syrian, Greeke,* or *Latine.*" There was one standard—the MT; and, if there are problems in their handling of it, these tend to reflect an inadequate knowledge of Hebrew rather than a departure from the text itself.

At about the same time the *KJV* was published, a Roman Catholic version was completed in the English College at Douay, France. The *Douay Bible* (1609-1610), or *Douay-Rheims* as the whole version was called, followed the dictum of the Council of Trent in 1546 (as well as the custom of John Wycliffe) in using the Latin Vulgate for its authoritative text. Although the Vulgate came from the hand of St. Jerome, who was the prince among early biblical scholars and probably the only one who knew and used Hebrew, his translation followed the LXX in too many respects. This shortcoming continued in Roman Catholic Bibles down to the time of Ronald Knox and the early years following World War II, and has only been set right in the most modern Catholic Bibles.

From the seventh to the nineteenth centuries, while a good deal of work was being done on the NT text, little new material was brought to bear on the OT. In the heated controversies which set Dean William Burgon against the English revisers of the nineteenth century, little was said about the text of the OT. The reason is easy to see: the OT portion of the *English Revised Version (ERV)* of 1885 follows a text almost identical to that of the *KJV.* The revisers were equally conservative in their use of the VSS, although their reasons may have differed slightly. Similarly traditional in textual matters was an American counterpart to the *ERV*, the *American Standard Version (ASV)* of 1901, again in all major respects a literal translation of the ben Chayim text.

A new era began with the publication of the *Revised Standard Version (RSV)* of the complete Bible in 1952. Not only did the revisers break with an old but now dated tradition by using the 1937 *BH³* as their basic OT text, but they opened the door to a limited number of textual emendations, particularly where the LXX or another VS lent support. Even a few readings from the DSS of Isaiah were included, although little work on the textual reliability of Qumran material had been done at that time.[37] In general it should be noted that the *RSV*, despite its pioneering stance, remained reasonably conservative in its departure from the MT. A few conjectured readings lack support from the MSS or VSS,[38] but, in the main, readings not found in the MT are well supported and clearly marked in the footnotes.

Once the barn door had been opened, however, it almost seemed as though all the horses fled at once! A host of private and committee-produced translations have appeared since the *RSV*, some of which seem to treat the MT tradition with far less respect than previous custom. Chief among the major offerings may be listed the *New English Bible (NEB)* of 1965, and the Roman Catholic *Jerusalem Bible (JB)* of 1966.

The *NEB*, an ecumenical venture by the major British Church groups, is marked in the OT by a liberal use of conjectures, many of which represent the creative if not always judicious hand of the late Oxford scholar G. R. Driver. Professor Driver's introduction to the OT portion describes the procedure followed and the attitude taken to the text. While the translators used *BH³* as a basis, the MT "incorporated the mistakes of generations of copyists," and "many errors of later copyists also found their way into it." In order to recover the original Hebrew the VSS are made a particular court of appeal, beginning with the LXX and continuing down to the medieval Arab translations. Certain elements in the MT are set aside, including the Psalm headings as

---

37. For a brief summary see F. F. Bruce, *The English Bible: A History of Translations* (London: Lutterworth Press, 1961), pp. 191-93.

38. One thinks of Ps 2:11b-12a, "Serve the LORD with fear, with trembling kiss his feet." See below for further discussion of this text.

"almost certainly not original," and the order of verses is sometimes changed (e.g., Job 41:1-6 follow 39:30). Emendations are recorded in the notes, however, "except where only the vowels are affected." A notable additional feature, though not directly a textual matter, is the widespread use of cognate languages, which are employed to find a fresh meaning for the consonantal text; although the conjectural emendations are always noted, some of these virtually conjectured interpretations are not.

If the *NEB* OT represents a Protestant willingness to throw textual caution to the winds, the *Jerusalem Bible (JB)* shows that Catholic scholars can at least follow the same inclination. Produced originally in 1956 under the aegis of French Dominicans in Jerusalem, the English translation of 1966 was made largely from the Hebrew and Greek texts. This in itself represents a departure from the *Douay-Rheims* tradition, but more to the point for text critics is the free use of readings from the VSS (especially the LXX) and from pure conjecture. Like the *RSV* and *NEB*, the *JB* is provided with a fine set of notes to explain the variants, although for the beginner the changes can be rather confusing. Not only are variant readings freely adopted, but phrases considered "glosses" (explanatory notes in the MT; e.g., "and the rest stayed behind," 1 Sam 30:9) are omitted, and, like the *NEB*, the order of the verses is sometimes altered (e.g., Amos 5:7 is placed after v. 9). Certainly the translators of the *JB*, like those of the *NEB*, feel that the emendations better represent the original than slavish reproduction of the MT, and the task of the text critic is ultimately to make that kind of decision. The reader, however, should be aware that these translations do represent a departure from long tradition, a change which still has not attained the status of consensus among experts in the field.

A second Roman Catholic translation, the *New American Bible (NAB)* of 1970, follows many of the same textual principles as the *JB*, though without the convenient textual notes at the bottom of the page. For the specialist, however, an appendix is available to furnish a guide to alternate readings. In addition, the preface helpfully lists the particular books in which the MT has been widely corrected (e.g., 1 and 2 Samuel), supplanted (Psalms), or rearranged (Job, Proverbs).

The appendix to the *NAB* is but one of several textual guides available for sorting out the readings in recent translations. The text critic will find, in addition to scattered articles by G. R. Driver on such matters, a definitive list of *NEB* readings and their support (though little else) in L. H. Brockington, *The Hebrew Text of the Old Testament: The Readings Adopted by the Translators of the New English Bible.*[39] For other helpful comparisons of questionable texts and how the *RSV, NEB, JB* (in its French dress), and others have handled them, two publications among many produced by the United Bible Societies (London) may be mentioned. *Old Testament Translation Problems,*[40] by A. R. Hulst and others, deals primarily with translation but also comments on the text followed by the *RSV* and the *Dutch New Version. Preliminary and Interim Report on the Hebrew Old Testament Text Project,*[41] by D. Barthelémy and others, compares readings in the *RSV, NEB, JB* (French), and the *Revised Luther Bible* (German) where these depart from the MT. The initial volume, which covers only the Pentateuch, gives full supporting data for each reading, makes a graded choice in each case (A, B, C, D), and gives the rules in codified form by which the text was chosen. Though designed for the translator in the field, such a help can be used with great profit by any student of Hebrew, and is increasingly required as the textual scene becomes more complex.

Two recent translations by evangelical scholarship have generally resisted the trend toward a more eclectic text. Certainly the *New American Standard Bible (NASB)*, published in full in 1971, represents the most consistent return to the earlier practice. Although the support of the VSS is set out in the footnotes for an occasional departure from the MT, the preface speaks only of "the latest edition of Rudolph Kittel's *Biblia Hebraica* . . . together with the most recent light from lexicography, the cognate languages, and the Dead Sea Scrolls." In fact, the *NASB* functions largely as a reasonably literal rendering (what students some-

39. L. H. Brockington, *The Hebrew Text of the Old Testament: The Readings Adopted by the Translators of the New English Bible* (Oxford: Oxford University Press; Cambridge: Cambridge University Press, 1973). D. F. Payne ("Old Testament Textual Criticism: Its Principles and Practice," *Tyndale Bulletin* 25 [1974]:99-112) has criticized Brockington for providing so little information, and undertaken a general critique of text-critical methods employed by modern English versions.

40. A. R. Hulst, *Old Testament Translation Problems*, Helps for Translators 1 (Leiden: E. J. Brill, 1960).

41. D. Barthélemy et al., *Preliminary and Interim Report on the Hebrew Old Testament Text Project* (London: United Bible Societies, 1973-).

times call a "pony") of the MT as represented in *BH³*. The *New International Version (NIV)*, by contrast, seeks to follow a somewhat broader path. The preface affirms the use of the MT as a base except where the MT "seemed doubtful and where accepted principles of textual criticism showed that one or more of these textual witnesses [LXX, SP, etc.] appeared to provide the correct reading." No criteria have yet been provided on how these are to be weighted, but the *NIV* in general indicates a much more conservative handling of such variants than one has come to expect in translations like the *NEB, JB,* and *NAB*.

Another major edition of Scripture was completed in 1977 with the publication of the entire *Good News Bible (GNB,* or *Today's English Version, TEV)*, which follows a fairly standard approach to the text. A preface affirms that the OT portion is based on *BH³*, with freedom to take the readings from the *qere,* from new understandings of the consonantal text, or from other Hebrew MSS or the VSS, in that order. In practice, as a brief perusal of the apparatus will show, use of the VSS and conjectural emendation has in places been widespread. But these variants are clearly indicated by the footnotes, and in a popular translation a bit more freedom may more readily be accepted.

KINDS OF TEXTUAL ERRORS

Changes or errors in the text may be classified under various headings. Some errors were caused by a simple misunderstanding of the text (e.g., wrong vowels or faulty word division), while others actually corrupted it (e.g., omission of a line). Again, most errors resulted from unintentional copy mistakes, while others came about in a well-meaning attempt to improve the text. In the following survey, the intention of the copyist will provide the dividing line for classifying textual errors, a system followed by the majority of studies on the subject. The examples presented merely illustrate the kinds of changes which text critics find. It will be readily seen that the vast majority are of minor import, a fact, however, that does nothing to diminish the need for achieving the best possible text.

Unintentional Changes

Confusion of sounds or letters. Whether a text was copied by looking at the original or hearing it read aloud, the possibility of confusion was always present. At different periods Hebrew employed two different scripts, and within each script certain letters looked very much alike. And of course, there are always some sounds that are easily confused with others. For example, both the earlier Paleo-Hebrew and the later square scripts employed *resh* and *daleth* characters ("r" and "d") which were very similar in shape and appearance (in square script, ר and ד respectively). Thus, comparing Gen 10:4 with 1 Chr 1:7, we are not surprised to find Rodanim in one and Dodanim in the other. Because the place mentioned is part of Javan, or Greece (the list is a table of nations rather than individuals), we suspect that modern Rhodes is in view and prefer to read Rodanim.

A more complex example comes from Amos 9:12, where the Hebrew text says "that they may possess [*yyršw*] the remnant of Edom." The passage is quoted in Acts 15:17 and generally follows the LXX, but with quite a different result: here it says "that the rest of men may seek the Lord." Working back from the Greek to the Hebrew text on which it is apparently based, it is clear that the text was read with the verb "seek" (*ydršw*) rather than "possess" (*yyršw*). This may have been a matter of confusing two letters (although *yodh* and *daleth* are not that much alike), or it may have been a matter of two verbs that sounded much alike. As there are other difficulties in this verse, any attempt to correct the reading must take the whole into account, but the above will serve to illustrate the initial point.

Incorrect vocalization. Inasmuch as the vowel letters were not added finally until the Masoretic period, and even the *matres lectionis* were a relatively recent innovation, there was plenty of potential for error. Basic to many readings in the *NEB* is the idea that not only was there confusion in Masoretic copying, but that already before the Masoretes the original vocalization of early Hebrew words had passed from use and been forgotten. Thus G. R. Driver and others have felt free to search in the lexica of cognate languages for words of the same consonants that might with a new vocalization supply the lost meaning. Setting aside some of this practice as extreme and lacking in external control, we can still find in it much food for creative thought.

In any case, vowel patterns could be easily confused. In

Isa 7:11, for example, where the MT reads "Make the request deep . . . ," almost all modern translations (including the textually conservative *NASB*) change "request" (*šĕ'ālāh*) to "Sheol" (*šĕ'ōlāh*) to read "let it be deep as Sheol" in parallel to the next phrase "or high as heaven." In either case, the four consonants *š'lh* are undisturbed.

Again, in the Amos 9:12 passage referred to above, the word "Edom" (*'ĕdôm*) is rendered in the LXX by the Greek equivalent of "man" (Heb. *'ādām*) and quoted that way in Acts 15:17. In the consonantal text "Edom" (*'dwm*) and "man" (*'dm*) were identical before the *mater lectionis waw* ("w") was added, and the two were at some point confused.

Omission. The most common omissions in copying came about when the scribe permitted his eye to rest on letters similar to those he was expecting but further down the line. Thus, for example, in Judg 20:13, from an original line *wl"bwbnybnymn* ("and the sons of Benjamin were not willing"), one of the two sequences *bny* ("sons of") has been omitted, leaving *wl"bwbnymn* — "and Benjamin [sing.] were not willing [pl.]."

Another common error results when similar endings in nearby phrases or lines cause a scribe's eye to skip over to the second and miss an entire phrase or more. In the LXX of 1 Sam 14:41, a further passage is found after "Saul said, 'O LORD God of Israel." It reads: "Why hast thou not answered thy servant this day? If this guilt is in me or in Jonathan my son, O LORD, God of Israel, give Urim; but if this guilt is in thy people Israel. . . ." It is obvious that the scribe's eye skipped from the first "Israel" to the third. As a result, the continuation in the MT was afterward wrongly vocalized as "Give perfect" (*tāmîm*) to try to make sense of what remained, whereas with the last phrase of the longer passage it nicely completes the prayer of Saul as "give Thummim" (*tummîm*, from the same root). It is perhaps a significant indication of method that almost all modern translations (except *NASB*) follow the LXX here.

Addition. The reverse of the previous problem also occurs. A probable example is found in 2 Kgs 18:17 where the sequence *wyy'lw wyyb'w* ("and they went up and came") follows *both* references to Jerusalem in the MT. The second sequence is absent from the ancient VSS, and when present adds nothing to the sense. Most modern translations (except *NASB*) relegate the addition to a footnote. Examples can be multiplied, and are usually easy enough to spot.

Transposition. An instance of simple transposition (reversal) of two letters, corrected in the LXX and all modern versions except *NASB*, is found in Ps 49:11 (MT v. 12). The consonantal text has *qrbm* ("their inner parts" or "thoughts"), while the LXX translates '"their graves," clearly from the Hebrew word *qbrm*. The MT as it stands defies a reasonable solution, though a valiant attempt to preserve the consonantal text can be seen in the Anchor Bible — "inside their external home."[42] But following the LXX and making the simple emendation restores unity to the entire passage. It should be noted that this kind of correction is made without any kind of major dislocation in the text, and also with full support from the ancient VSS. By contrast, the transposition of whole lines of this psalm by the *NEB* translators is neither required by the context nor supported by any witness in antiquity.

Another case of more radical surgery, also without support from ancient witnesses, is found in the way the *RSV* and *JB* avoid the problematic word for "son" (*bar,* an Aramaic word which would not normally appear in a Hebrew psalm) in Ps. 2:11b-12a. By shifting the consonants for "rejoice" (*KJV*) to a position after those for "son," the psalm now reads, "with trembling kiss his feet" (MT *wgylw br'dh nšqw-br* has been reconstructed as *br'dh nšqw brglyw*). Such conjectures can be judged by whether the method of solution is really less problematic than the original problem.

Gloss. This category may, of course, include intentional corrections to the text, though most marginal glosses were probably incorporated into the text itself only by mistake. Explanatory glosses were also probably part of the earliest form of the written text, such as the phrase "which is the eighth month" in 1 Kgs 6:38; it clarifies for a later generation what is meant by the old Canaanite month name Bul. Because so many so-called glosses in

42. Dahood, *Psalms I*, p. 298.

the text may fit this category, a policy of caution is best adopted; there is no reason, for example, to eliminate harmless glosses to the extent the *JB* seems to have done in many places (e.g., 1 Sam 30:9; 31:7). Of a different order is the suggested transposition of a possibly misplaced, and therefore misleading, gloss in Gen 10:4; inasmuch as it is known that the Philistines came from Caphtor (Amos 9:7), while nothing is known of the Casluhim, the *JB, NEB, GNB,* and *NAB* (the latter without a footnote) all transpose "from which the Philistines came" to follow "Caphtor." Again, this is not a question of whether the gloss is original or desirable; in fact, it is highly informative. The question is rather whether in its present place the gloss is misleading. But since we do not know anything about the Casluhim, it is always possible that the gloss would apply to them as much as to the Caphtorim, and so the text is probably best left as it is (so *RSV, NASB*), perhaps with the addition of a footnote.

Other glosses, too, are generally best left alone, unless there is clear MS support for their deletion. Hos 14:9, for example, seems to function as a later hortatory comment rather than a word from the prophet, but its place in the text is now well attested and to remove it would be precarious, at least on textual grounds.

Incorrect division. Ancient texts were often written without word division, a practice which presented many possibilities for erroneous reading. A widely accepted emendation deriving from this situation, though lacking textual support from other MSS or VSS (the LXX is totally different), is found in Amos 6:12. The problematic question "Does one plow with oxen?" (cf. *KJV, NASB*), which in the context requires a negative answer, can be emended to a much more understandable "Does one plow the sea with oxen?" (so *RSV*) simply by dividing *bbqrym* into *bbqr ym*. No injustice is done to the text, and the required answer follows.

Intentional Changes

We have already noted that most changes result from normal human error. A few, however, may be traced to well-meaning attempts on the part of a scribe to correct what he saw as a faulty or unclear statement. Many of these were merely modernizations of spelling or grammar, or filling out missing subjects and objects.

These need not concern us further. Most of them become apparent only when comparing texts and VSS rather than appraising a problem in the MT. Those that do concern us are the attempts to harmonize or conflate two accounts, or to remove difficult or objectionable expressions. Such activity can be discerned most readily by comparing other MSS and VSS, and the rules of text criticism (given below) will help determine a probable original reading.

Harmonization and expansion. More significant than the number of times when parallel accounts have been harmonized is the number of times when they have not. Apparently little attempt was made to adjust data in Chronicles to that in Samuel-Kings or vice versa. The possibility nevertheless exists and must be faced when it is evident. More easily determined are the places where the text has been expanded, usually evident through comparison with other MSS and VSS. The shorter versions of the LXX forms of Job and Jeremiah have long been noted, and now evidence from Qumran shows that expansion or contraction was not limited to the one book. To the DSS and the LXX may be compared the SP and of course the MT. Which text form is to be preferred and why a text has been expanded are complicated questions,[43] but it may no longer be taken for granted that the MT is always best, especially when it represents an obviously expansionist tendency.

Specific examples of harmonization include a scribal substitution of "sixth day" in the SP and LXX (followed by *NEB*) for the MT's first reference to "seventh day," a change obviously designed to fit the context better, though the *NASB*'s "By the seventh day . . ." is equally satisfactory. Of a somewhat different order is the attempt by some of the VSS (e.g., Vulgate) to bring 2 Sam 22:33 into line with the parallel text in Ps 18:32, changing the MT's "my strong fortress" to "who girds me with strength." That such tendencies can occur in all ages is evidenced by the *NASB*'s translation of Heb. *kōhănîm* (priests) as "chief ministers," a clear attempt to harmonize an embarrassing original with the parallel text in 1 Chr 18:17.[44]

43. See Klein, *Textual Criticism of the OT.*
44. For a better solution, see Carl E. Armerding, "Were David's Sons Really Priests?" in *Current Issues in Biblical and Patristic Interpretation*, ed. G. F. Hawthorne (Grand Rapids: Eerdmans, 1975), pp. 75-86.

Expansionist tendencies have been mentioned above, particularly in connection with the MT of Jeremiah. Additional examples could be cited, but the most obvious ones occur in some DSS and SP rather than in MT.

Conflation of two or more variant readings. Often cited is Ezek 1:20 (MT), in which two almost identical phrases appear in a setting that is difficult to explain as simple dittography (unintentional double writing). If the doublet was intentional it probably represents a conflation of two variant texts. The *NASB* and other modern translations relegate the duplication to a marginal note. Many other possibilities could be cited, but the topic becomes increasingly complex and the key question of intentionality is difficult to ascertain.[45]

Removal of difficult or objectionable expressions. A simple substitution of "Assyria" for the MT's "Ashdod" in the LXX of Amos 3:9 (cf. *NASB* with *RSV*) removes a logical irregularity in the verse. More difficult or objectionable to early copyists were references to cursing God (Job 1:5, 11; 2:5, 9), and all were altered in the MT to read "bless" (*brk*) instead, though modern translations consistently revert to the understood original, usually without even a footnote. Equally offensive, at least to the editors of 2 Samuel, were royal names incorporating the divine element *ba'al*, though originally the term probably lacked any reference to Canaanite or Phoenician gods who were so designated. In Hebrew, as in Canaanite, *ba'al* simply means "lord," and the Chronicler seemed content to leave Saul's family with *ba'al* names (Ishbaal, 1 Chr 8:33; Merib-baal, v. 34). By contrast, 2 Sam 2:8, as well as chaps. 4, 9, 16, and 19, all substitute *-bósheth* (shame, abomination) for the *ba'al* element. These kinds of intentional alterations are easy to detect and, in any case, represent an honest attempt by pious Israelites to honor both God and His Word.

RULES FOR TEXT CRITICISM

Since copyist errors follow standard patterns in all pretechno-

---

45. For additional data see S. Talmon, "Conflate Readings (OT)," *Interpreter's Dictionary of the Bible,* Supplementary Volume, pp. 170-73.

logical societies, the principles or rules for choosing alternate readings or correcting apparent discrepancies are not unique to OT study. What is unique is the amount and kind of textual or linguistic evidence available, two areas in which NT and OT text critics are faced with vastly differing possibilities. Here are four guidelines to help the beginner understand and evaluate the conclusions of translators and commentators who have the skills required for textual decision making.

Choose the best MS evidence available. This will usually be the MT, though at times the DSS or one of the VSS will be chosen by experts. Even the neophyte student should be aware of any tendencies evident in a translation, and it is always useful to have at hand an English Bible which follows the MT as closely as possible, such as the *KJV, ASV,* or *NASB.*

Prefer the shorter reading. Expansion and glossing is a natural human tendency, and often additions to the text are readily spotted for what they are. Where the evidence is conflicting, the human psychology that drives us to explain rather than condense may be called upon as one criterion for selecting an option.

Prefer the more difficult reading. Few writers or editors will intentionally set forth obscurities. Often, even in antiquity, it was possible for a scribe to be unaware of the original meaning or historical-cultural point of reference, and particularly so when a nonvocalized text was employed. In such situations, clarification is a natural response, especially when the scribe in question had before him a single copy, one which he may well have concluded was itself in error. Modern scholarship has, through the study of antiquity, revived many of the tools needed to understand a difficult original, tools that were not available to the copyist of antiquity. In any case, the attempt to understand the more difficult reading should be made before jumping to the easier, explanatory rendering.

Avoid conjectural readings wherever an alternative is possible. Modern commentaries, with their increased dependence on comparative Semitic philology, especially Ugaritic studies, have often been able to make sense of a difficult text for which even as recent a translation as the *RSV* reached for a conjectural reading. Retaining the consonantal text and assuming that vowels are less reliable, scholars like Mitchell Dahood[46] have found in cognate languages possible, though not always probable, explanations of hundreds of texts that had been emended by earlier scholars. Dahood undoubtedly overused the method, but did not thereby invalidate it.

SUMMARY

Text criticism remains a discipline largely pursued by experts because of its technical requirements. But with the proliferation of translations and the revival of the art of the commentator in our day, it behooves even the beginning student to know something about the procedures and methods. Since the discovery of the DSS, and in the light of the linguistic advances brought about since 1929 with the Ugaritic texts, there are now more possibilities for understanding the text than at any time since the days of the prophets. Grasping the simple principles outlined above should help us to sort out the bewildering array of claims and possibilities.

46. Cf., e.g., *Psalms I–III*, passim.

Index of Names

Abrahams, I., 28n
Ackroyd, P. R., 22n, 104n
Albright, W. F., 51n
Allis, O. T., 28n, 31, 35, 41n
Alonso-Schökel, L., 86, 89, 90
Anderson, A. A., 59n
Archer, G. L., 5n
Armerding, C. E., 124n
Astruc, J., 22

Bally, C., 69n
Baltzer, K., 56n, 57n
Barr, J., 5n, 73n, 86, 100n
Barthelémy, D., 118
Barthes, R., 69, 71, 72, 81, 85, 86ff., 90
Barton, D. M., 51n
Baskin, W., 69n
Beauchamp, P., 89, 95
Boudon, R., 70n
Bovon, F., 71n
Bowden, J., 51n
Bowie, W. R., 95n
Bowker, J., 102n
Brockington, L. H., 118
Brown, N., 94n, 95
Bruce, F. F., 116n
Burgon, W., 115

Calloud, J., 75n
Calvin, J., 4
Carruth, W. H., 43n

Cassuto, U., 28n, 31, 89
Childs, B. S., 19, 95n, 96
Chomsky, N., 71
Coats, G. W., 84, 91
Crespy, G., 93, 94
Cross, F. M., 104, 105
Culley, R. C., 74, 78-81, 84, 85, 88f., 92, 93
Cupitt, S. M., 43n

Dahood, M., 109, 122n, 127
Delitzsch, F., 1
Dibelius, M., 43
Driver, G. R., 116, 118, 120
Driver, S. R., 31, 34n, 39n, 40n

Eissfeldt, O., 22n, 51n
Elliger, K., 113n
Ellis, E. E., 106n
Engnell, I., 42n
Evans, C. F., 104n

Fokkelman, J. P., 84, 89ff., 95

Ginsburg, C. D., 106n, 112
Goldingay, J., 3, 46n
Good, E. M., 85f.
Gordis, R., 109n
Gordon, C. H., 28n
Goshen-Gottstein, M. H., 113
Graf-Wellhausen, 17, 28

Index of Names

Green, D. E., 56n
Green, W. H., 26n
Greenberg, M., 106n
Greimas, A. J., 74ff., 77, 78, 81, 87
Gressmann, H., 45
Gunkel, H., 43, 44, 45, 51, 55, 59, 87

Habel, N., 22f., 24n, 26, 27, 28f., 33f., 41n, 42, 86n
Harrison, R. K., 22n
Hartwell, H., 59n
Hawthorne, G. F., 124n
Hengstenberg, 45
Horner, T. M., 43n
Hort, F. J. A., 114
Hulst, A. R., 118

Jacobson, C., 76n
Jacobson, R., 69n, 70n, 87n
Jakobson, R., 69, 71, 81
Johnson, A. M., Jr., 71n

Kahle, P., 110n, 111n, 112, 113
Kantzer, K., 4n
Keil, C. F., 1, 45, 46
Kennicott, B., 112
Kessler, M., 84
Kidner, D., 26, 27, 60n
Kitchen, K. A., 18n, 48n, 57n
Klein, R. W., 103n, 105n, 124n
Kline, M. G., 18n, 64
Knox, R., 115
Koch, K., 43n, 44, 50, 51, 52, 55, 61n, 81n

Ladd, G. E., 17, 47n
Lampe, G. W. H., 104n
Leach, E., 71, 73, 78, 79, 81, 84, 88f.
Leiman, S. Z., 101n, 102n
Leupold, H. C., 26n
Levi-Strauss, C., 69, 70, 71, 72, 73, 74, 76ff., 78, 79, 80, 81, 85, 87, 88f., 94
Livingston, G. H., 52
Lyons, J., 71n

MacRae, D. G., 70n
Marks, J. H., 29n
Martin, W. J., 5n
McEvenue, S., 84
McNamara, M. J., 106n
Mendenhall, G. E., 57n
Miller, M. P., 106n
Montgomery, J. W., 4n
Morris, L., 12
Mowinckel, S., 45, 50n, 51, 54n, 59
Muilenburg, J., 84ff.

Orlinsky, H. M., 106n
Orr, J., 1

Packer, J. I., 4n
Patte, D., 73n, 74, 75f., 77f., 84
Payne, D. F., 118n
Piaget, J., 84f.
Polzin, R., 81-84, 85, 93, 95
Pritchard, J. B., 11n
Propp, V., 87
Purvis, J. D., 105n

von Rad, G., 6, 29, 31, 37f., 45n, 91
Rhodes, E. F., 100n
Ricoeur, P., 93, 94
Roberts, B. J., 100n, 104n, 105n, 106n, 107n, 108
Robertson, D., 86, 92n
Robinson, J. A. T., 47n
Rogerson, J. W., 69n, 71n, 88
de Rossi, J. B., 112
Rudolph, W., 113n
Rylaarsdam, J. C., 45n

Sarna, N., 24n
de Saussure, F., 69, 70
Sayce, A. H., 34f.
Schoepf, B. G., 76n
Sechehaye, A., 69n
Segal, M. H., 101n, 104n, 107n
Sheppard, G. T., 19n
Simpson, C. A., 95n
Skinner, J., 31n

Smith, G. A., 1
Snaith, N. H., 113
Soggin, J. A., 51n
Speiser, E. A., 11n
Spivey, R. A., 68n, 70, 71n, 72n, 73n, 94n, 95n
Stalker, D. M. G., 37n
Stigers, H. G., 26n

Talmon, S., 104n, 125n
Thompson, J. A., 18n
Tucker, G. M., 17f., 44, 45n, 51n, 52, 54, 55n, 92

Vaughan, M., 70n
Via, D. O., Jr., 73n
Visser-Hagedoorn, P., 84

Wagner, N. E., 24n

Walvoord, J. F., 4n
Warfield, B. B., 46
Weiner, H. M., 31n
Weiser, A., 51n, 59n
Weiss, M., 86
Wellhausen, J., 1, 2, 56, 96
Westcott, B. F., 15, 114
Westermann, C., 24, 61
White, H. C., 61n, 72n, 86, 87
Willis, J. T., 42n
Wilson, J. A., 11n
Wilson, R. D., 46
Wiseman, D. J., 5n
Wolf, H. M., 64
Woolf, B. L., 43n
Wright, G. E., 6
Würthwein, E., 100n, 107n, 109
Wycliffe, J., 115

Young, E. J., 5n, 26n

Scripture References

Genesis

1	17, 23, 24f., 26f., 28f., 30, 34, 38, 40, 89	6:5-8	30	9:18-29	30f.
		6:9	40	9:28-29	31
		6:9-22	30	9:36	35
1 – 3	13	6:14-16	35	10:1	40
1 – 4	31, 39, 88f.	7 – 9	31	10:4	120, 123
1 – 9	29	7:1-5	30	11	26
1 – 11	47, 48	7:6	30	11:1-9	90f.
1:1 – 2:3	24	7:7-8	30	11:7	91
1:26-28	40	7:9	30, 31	11:9	90
2	17, 24, 26f., 28f., 34, 38, 40	7:10	30	12	33, 51, 52, 54, 55, 82f.
		7:11	30		
2 – 4	40	7:12	30, 31	12 – 20	83
2:1-3	23	7:13-16a	30	12:10-20	34, 50
2:3	24	7:16	31, 35	19:30-38	81
2:4	24, 40	7:16a	31	20	33f., 51, 52, 54, 55, 82f.
2:4a	40	7:16b	31		
2:4b	24	7:16b-17	30	20:1-17	50
2:4-25,	24f.	7:18-21	30	20:18	34
2:4 – 4:26	30	7:22-23	30	24:15 – 30:24	31
3	29f.	7:24	30	25 – 35	90
3 – 4	24f.	8:1-2a	30	26	33, 51, 52, 54, 55, 82f.
3:17-19	40	8:2b	30		
4	30, 41	8:3-5	30	26:1-13	50
4:17-26	40, 41	8:6-12	30	26:24	34
4:25	30, 40	8:13a	30	28:10-22	90
5	30, 40, 41	8:13b	30	32:22-32	86ff.
5:1	40	8:14-19	30	32:23-32	71f.
5:1-3	40	8:20-21	35	32:24-32	65
5:28-31	40	8:20-22	30	32:32	65
5:29	40	9:1-17	30	37 – 47	91
6 – 9	30, 31f., 35	9:12-16	35	37:24	95n
6:1-4	30f.	9:18-27	31	38	81

Exodus			II Samuel			Job		
1 – 15		86	2:8		125	1:5		125
14		9f.	4		125	1:11		125
14:14		10	7		32, 38	2:5		125
15		8, 9f.	7:16		38	2:9		125
15:22-26		80	8		32	39:30		117
17:1-7		80	9		125	41:1-6		117
20		37	10		32			
20:22 – 23:19		36	11 – 12		32	Psalms		
20:24-36		36	13 – 20		32	1		49
24:7		36	16		125	2		59ff.
25 – 31		36	19		125	2:11b-12a		116n,
27		36f.	22		32			122
27:1-8		36	22:33		124	18		32
30		36f.	24		32	18:32		124
30:1-5		36				19	49, 50f., 54, 59	
32 – 34		39	I Kings			49:11 (MT 12)		122
34:6-7		38, 39	6:38		122			
			8		2	Isaiah		
Numbers			11:29-40		61	7:11		121
22		48f.	17:17-24		80	45:1		2
			21:18-19		61	51:10		7
						55:11		8
Deuteronomy			II Kings					
12 – 26		39	2:19-22		80	Jeremiah		
17:14-20		2	4:1-7		80	9:21		108
24:16		38, 39	4:38-41		80	20:19		8
25:19		108	6:25		109n	31:29-30		38
			18:17		121			
Joshua			I Chronicles			Ezekiel		
24		57f.	1:7		120	1:20		125
24:1-27		57	8:33		125	18:3		38
24:2		47	8:34		125	18:4		38
			17		32, 38	18:20		38
Judges			17:14		38			
3:11		46	18		32	Hosea		
3:30		46	18:17		124	8:14b		32
5:14		101	19		32	14:9		123
5:31		46	21		32			
8:28		46	22		33	Amos		
20:13		121	23 – 29		33	2:5		32
						3:9		125
			II Chronicles			4:1a		61
I Samuel			36		33	4:1b		61
14:41		121				4:1-3		62
30:9		117, 123	Ezra			4:2a		61
31:7		123	7:6		101	4:2b-3		61

Scripture References

4:12	62	Luke		II Timothy	
5:1-17	49, 62	1:2	47	3:16	14
5:7	117	10:30-35	74ff.		
5:8-9	62	24:44	102		
5:9	117			Hebrews	
6:12	123	Acts		1:1	14f.
7 – 9	62	4:25	59n	1:5	59n
7:14-17	61	4:25-26	59n		
9:7	123	13:33	59n		
9:12	120, 121	15:17	120, 121	II Peter	
				1:21	15
Jonah		I Corinthians			
1:2	8	15:3-7	47		
				Revelation	
Ecclesiasticus		Galatians		2:27	59n
44 – 50	102	1:1-10	74, 76ff.	19:15	59n